JURASSIC WORLD

THE OFFICIAL COLORING BOOK

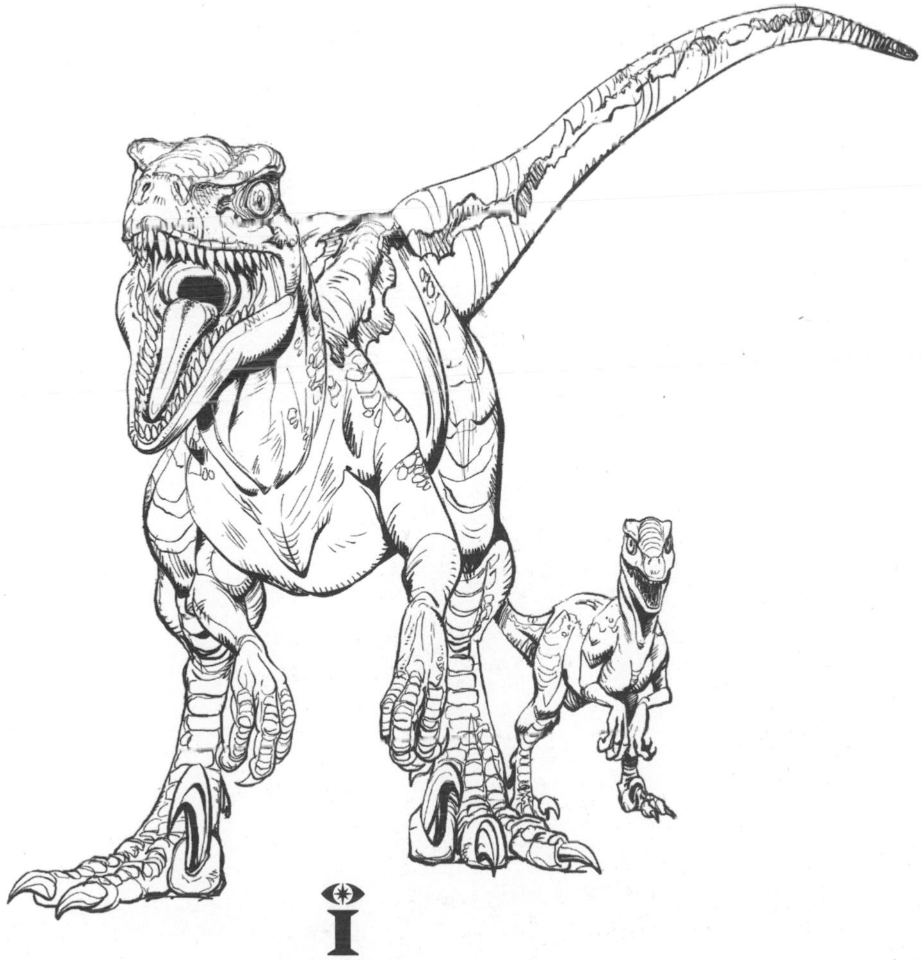

INSIGHT
EDITIONS

SAN RAFAEL • LOS ANGELES • LONDON

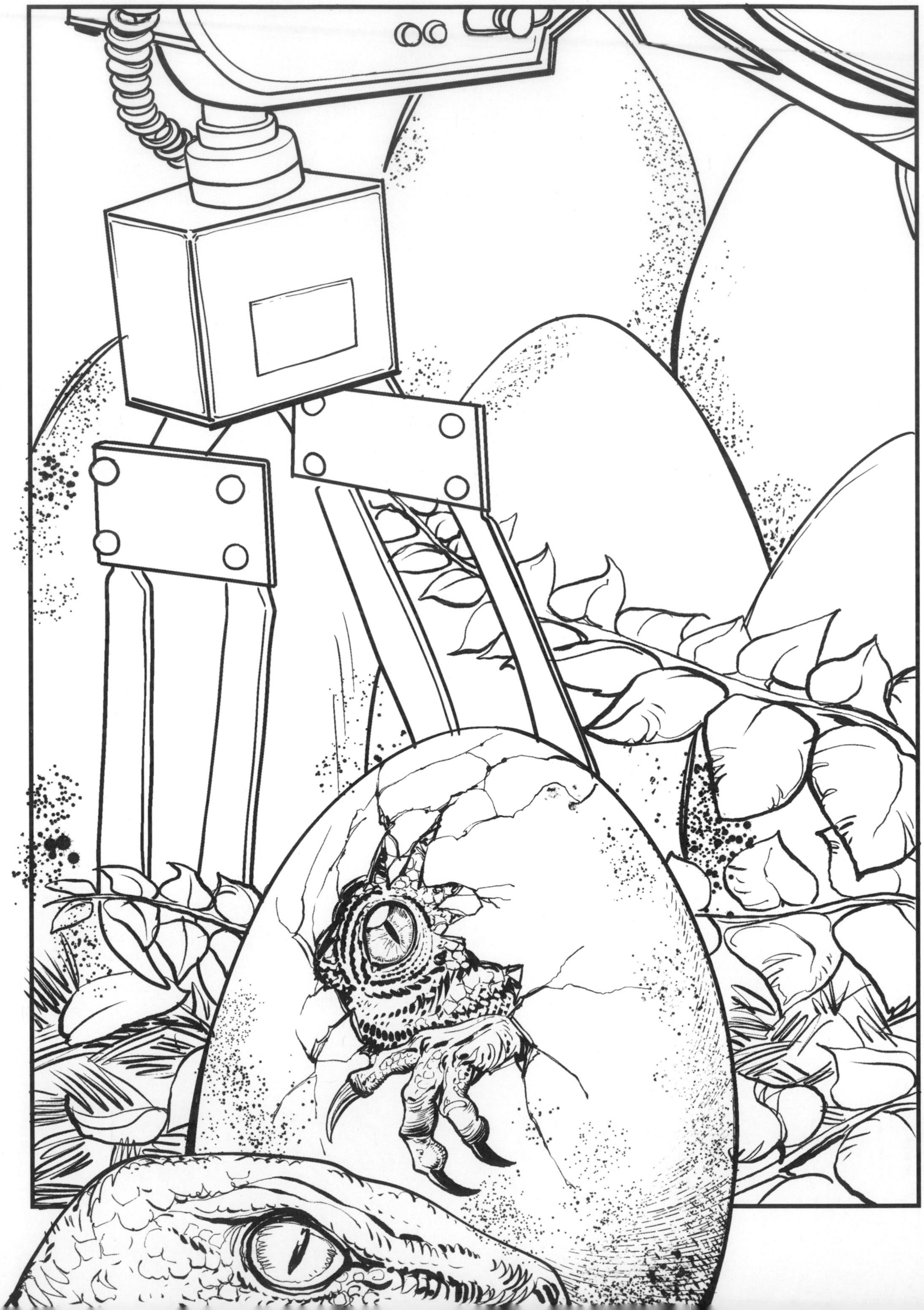

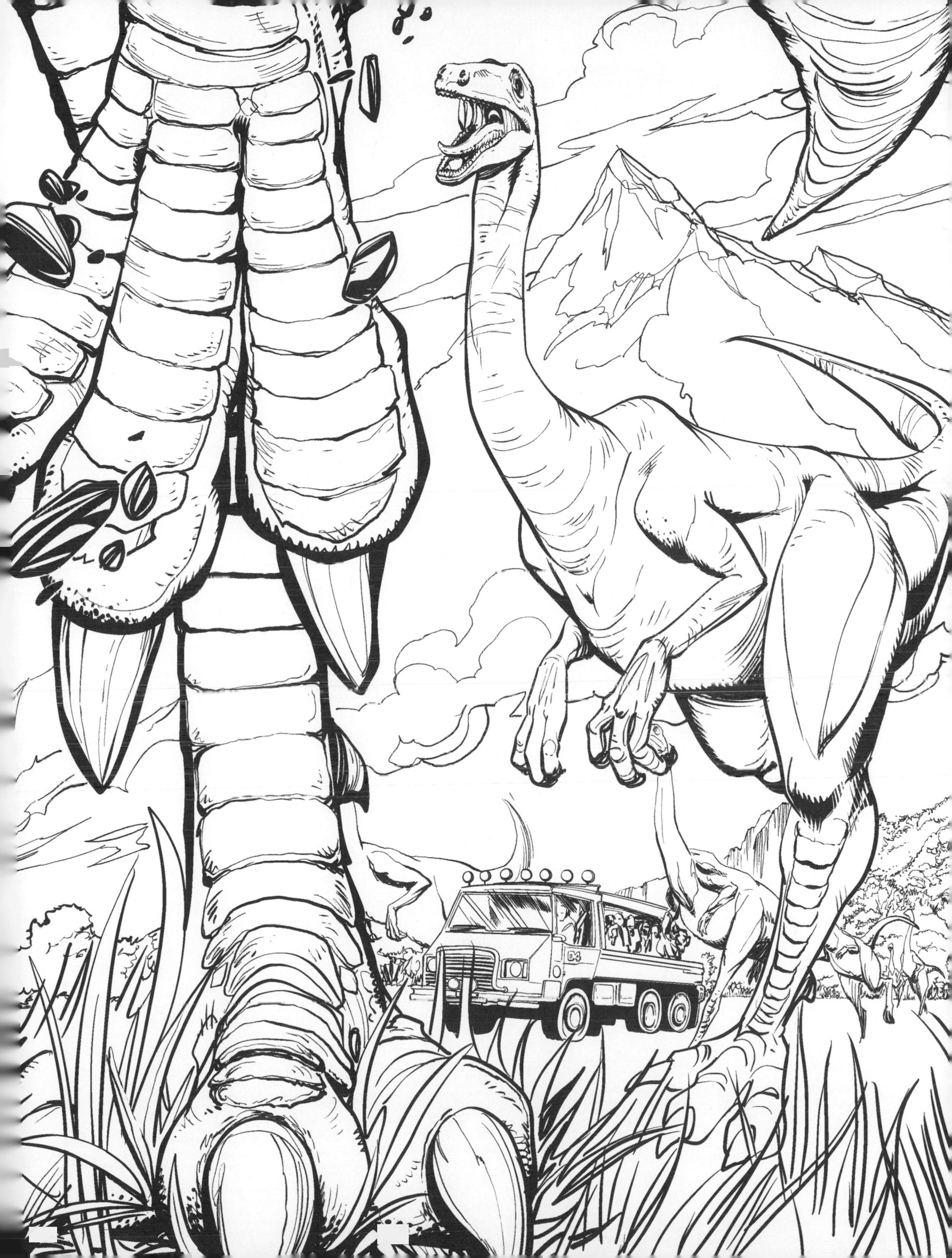
04

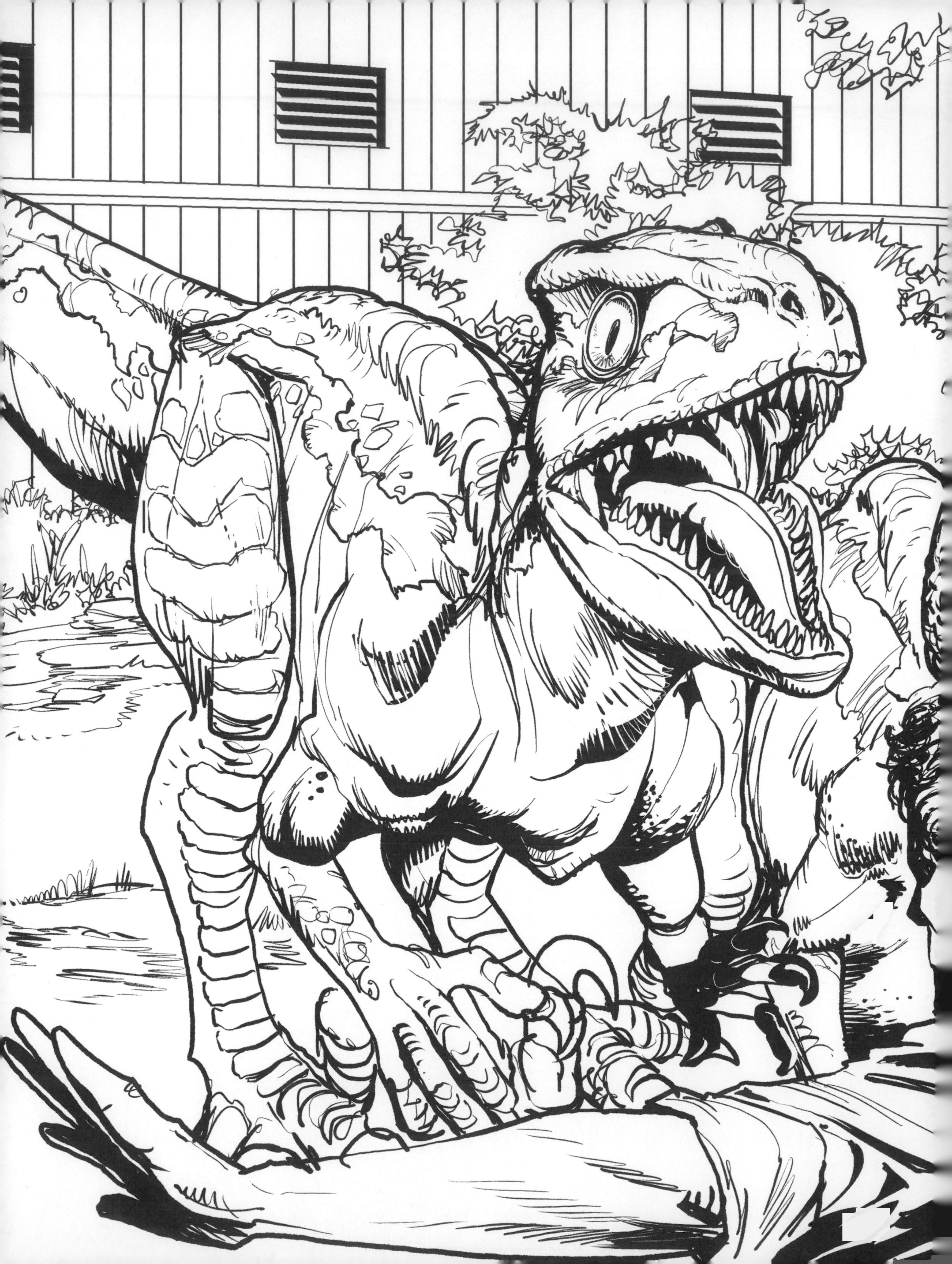

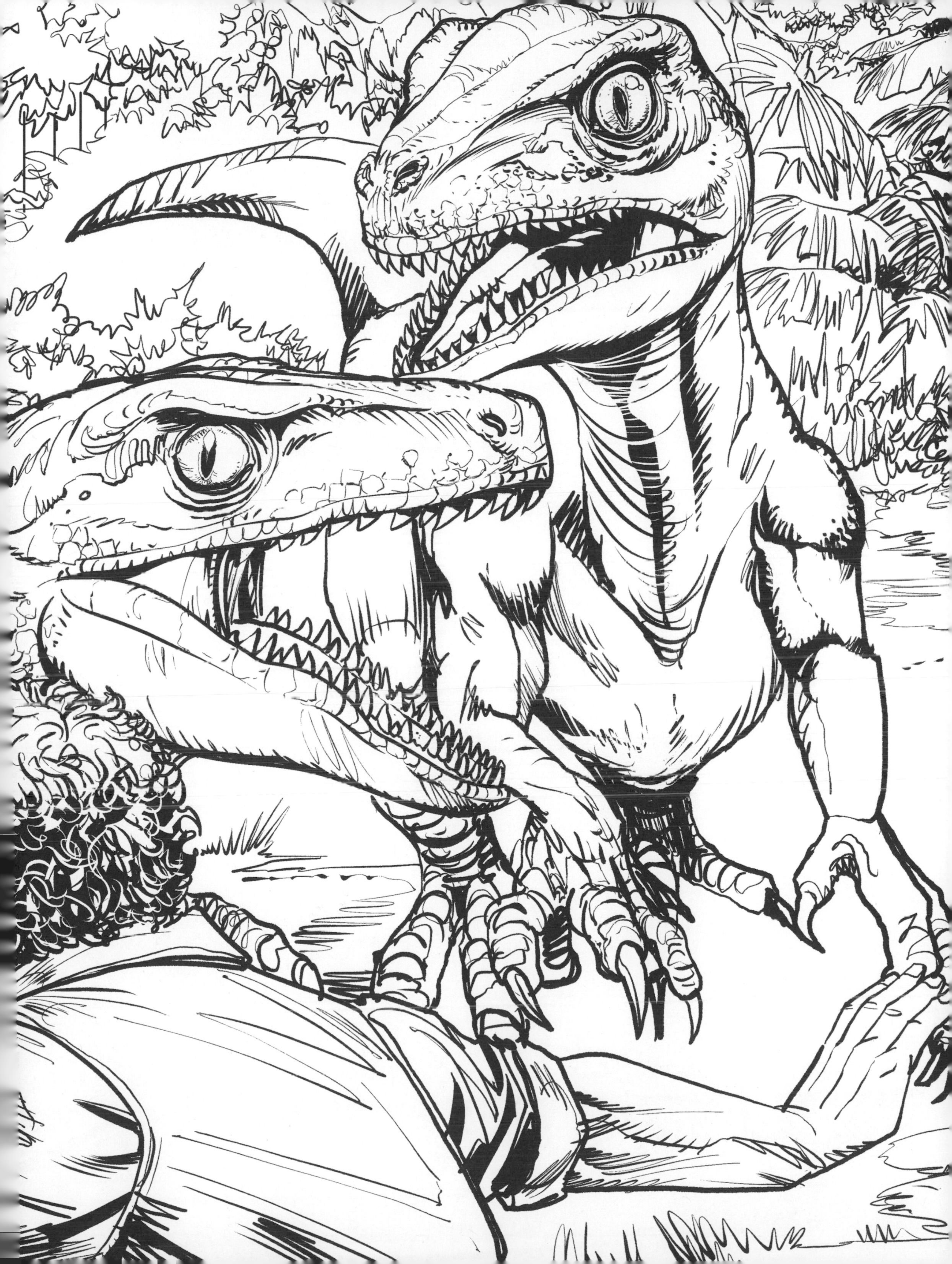

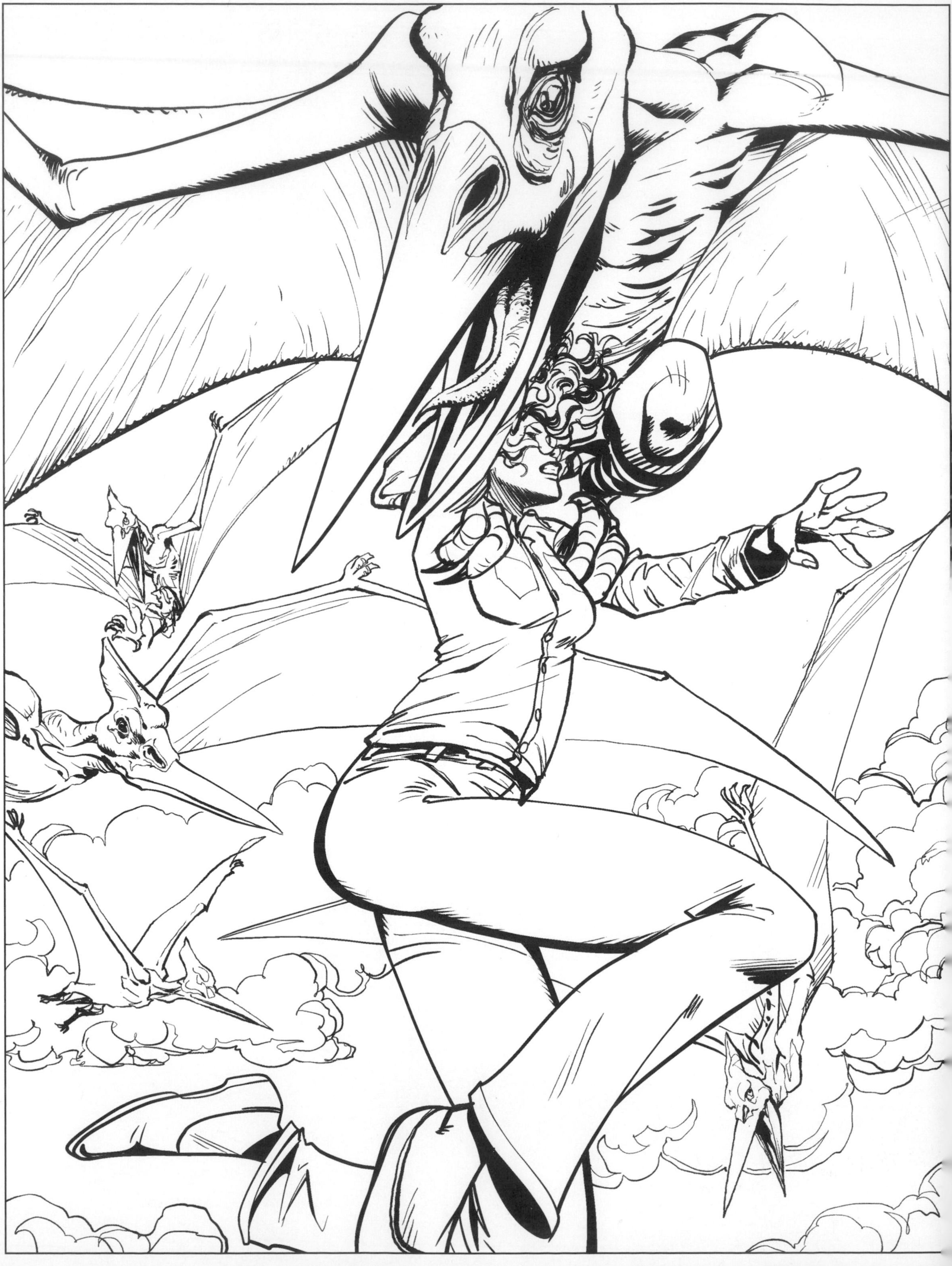

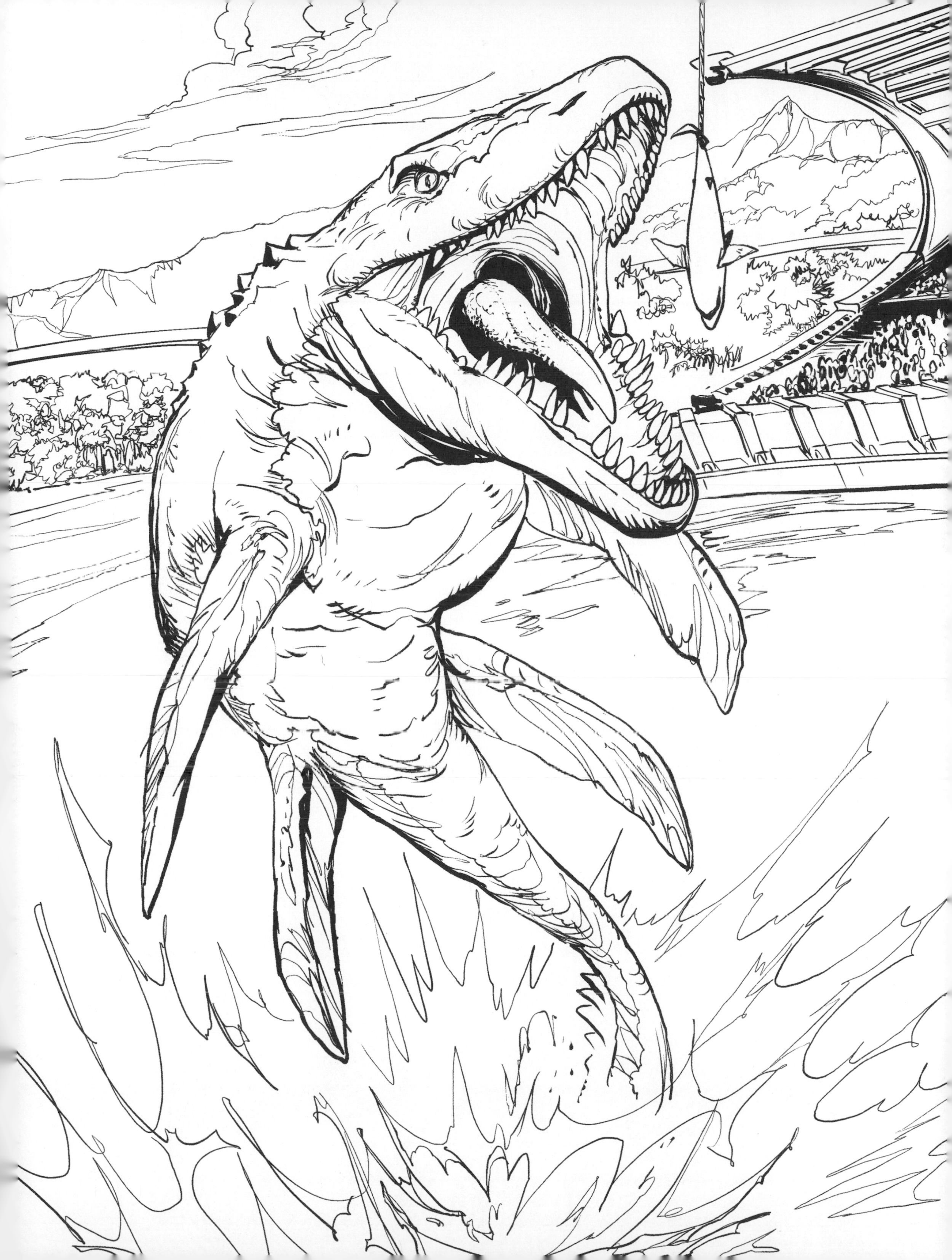

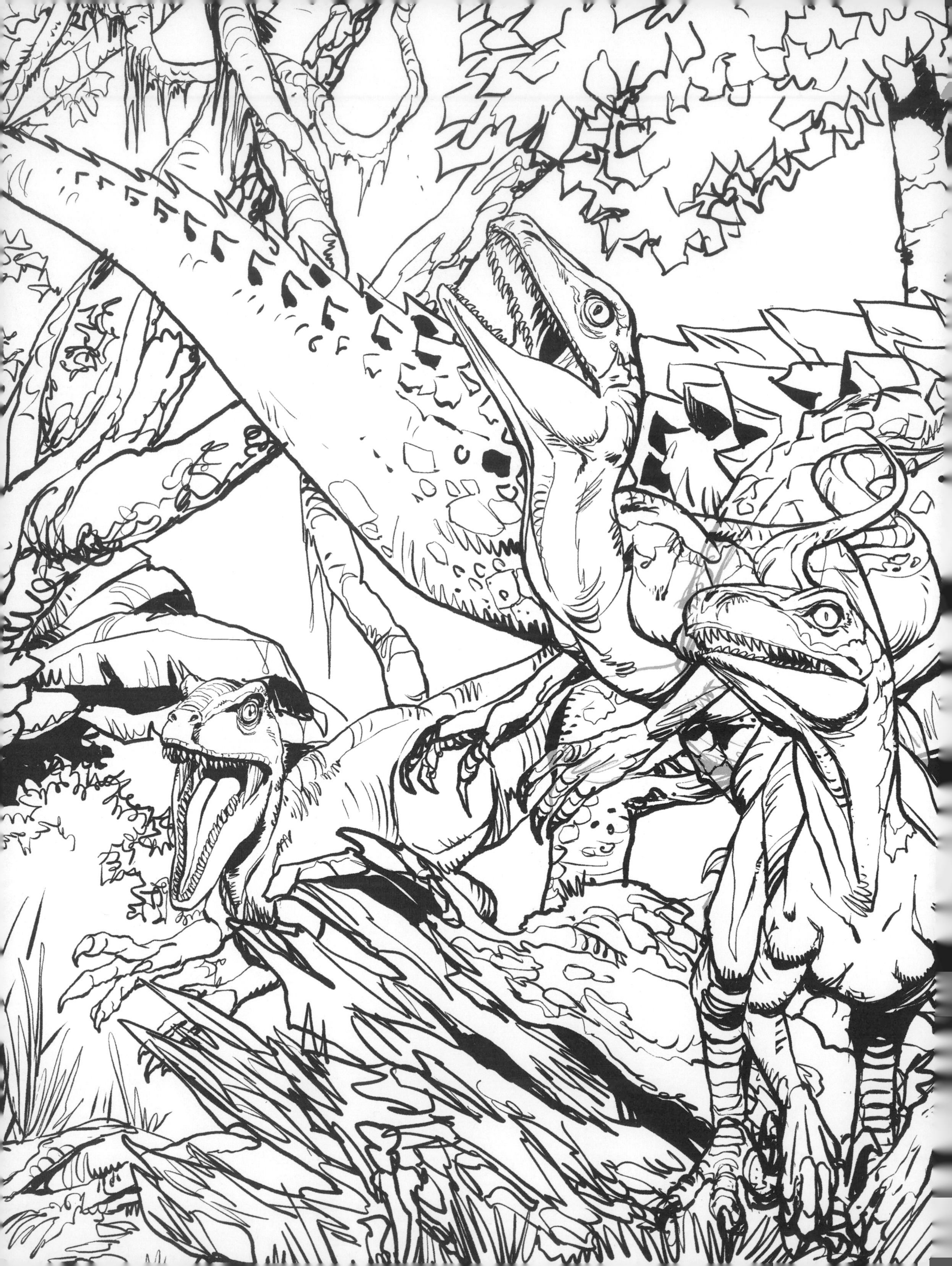

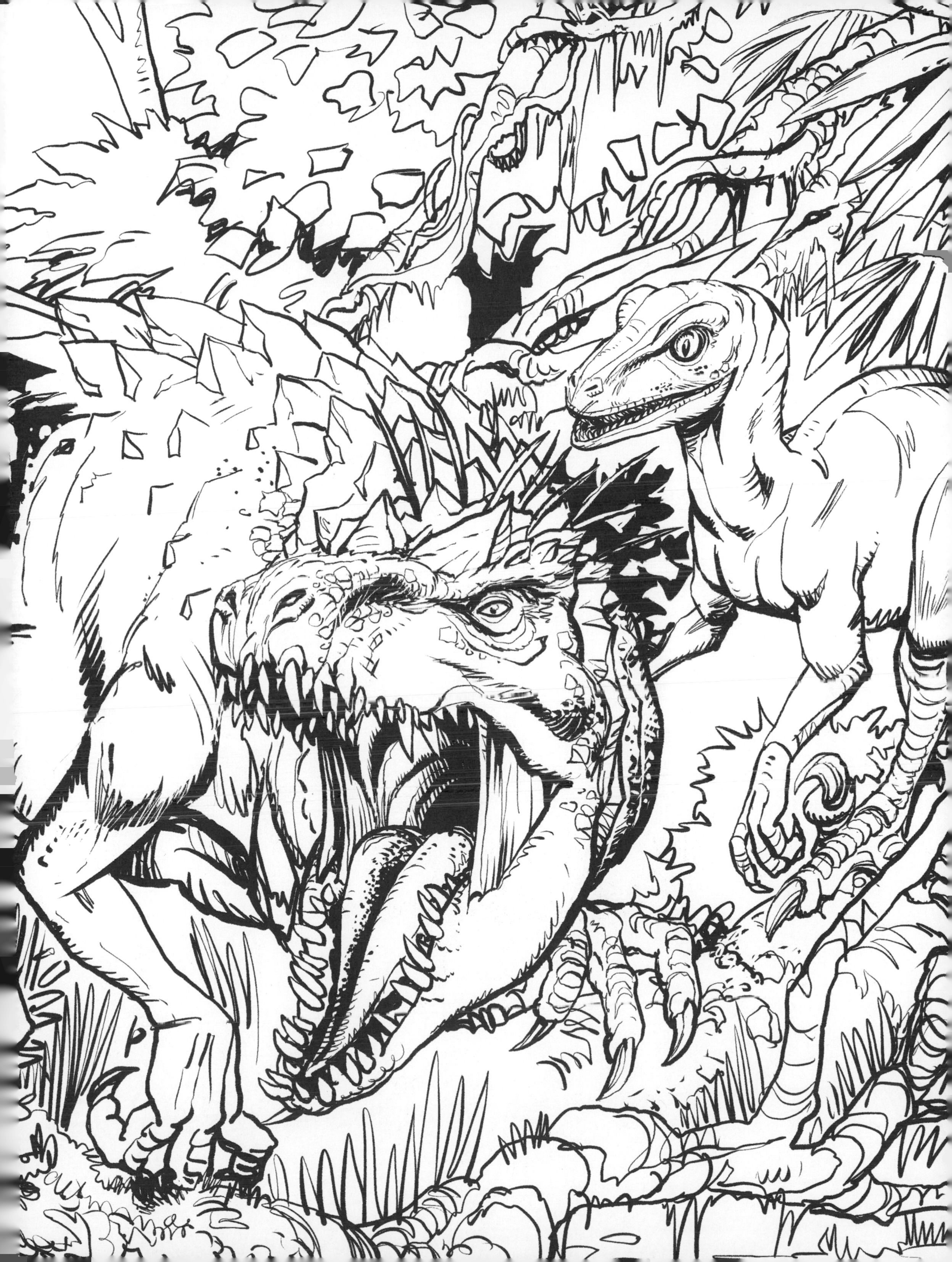

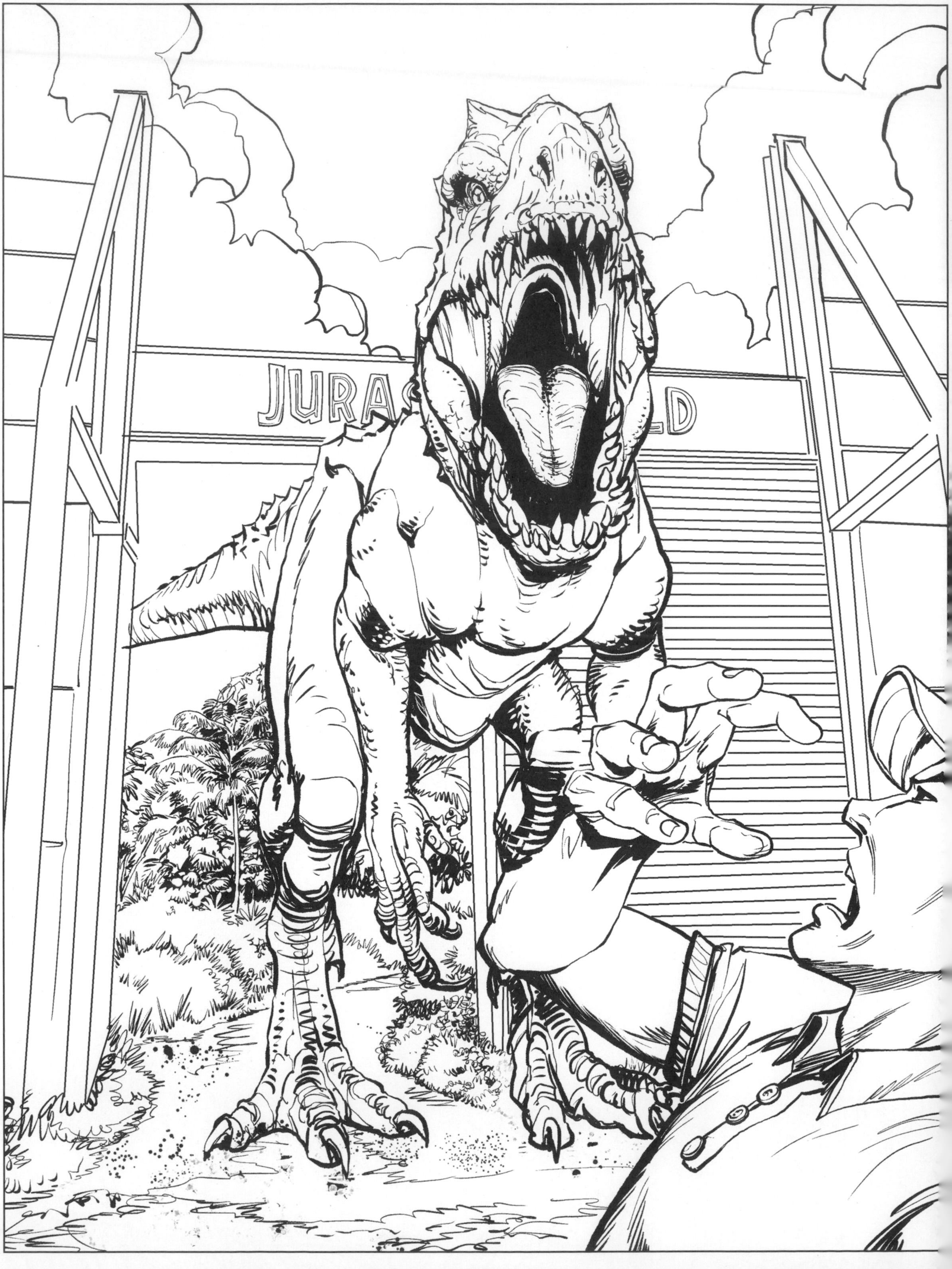
JURAS
LD

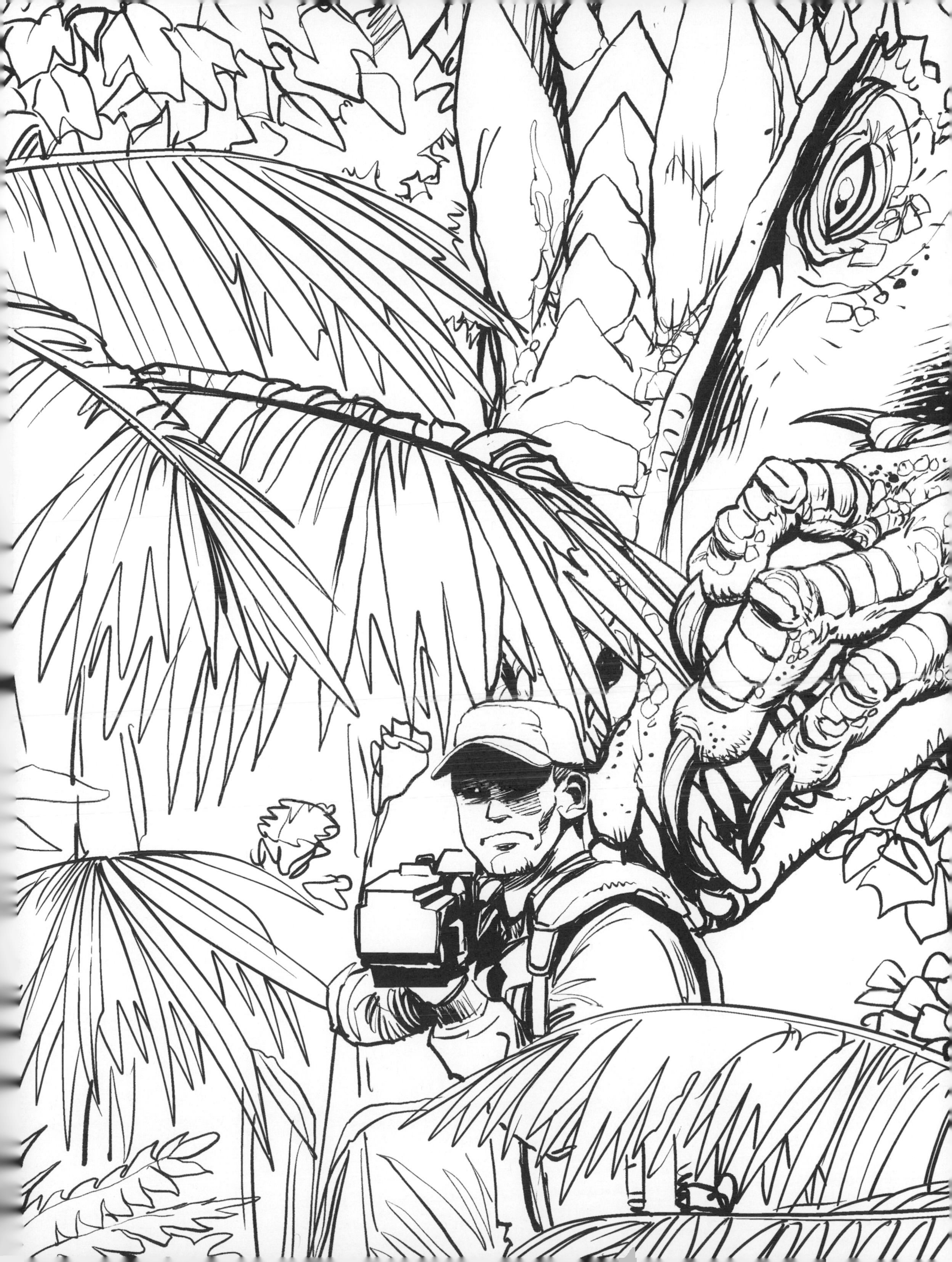

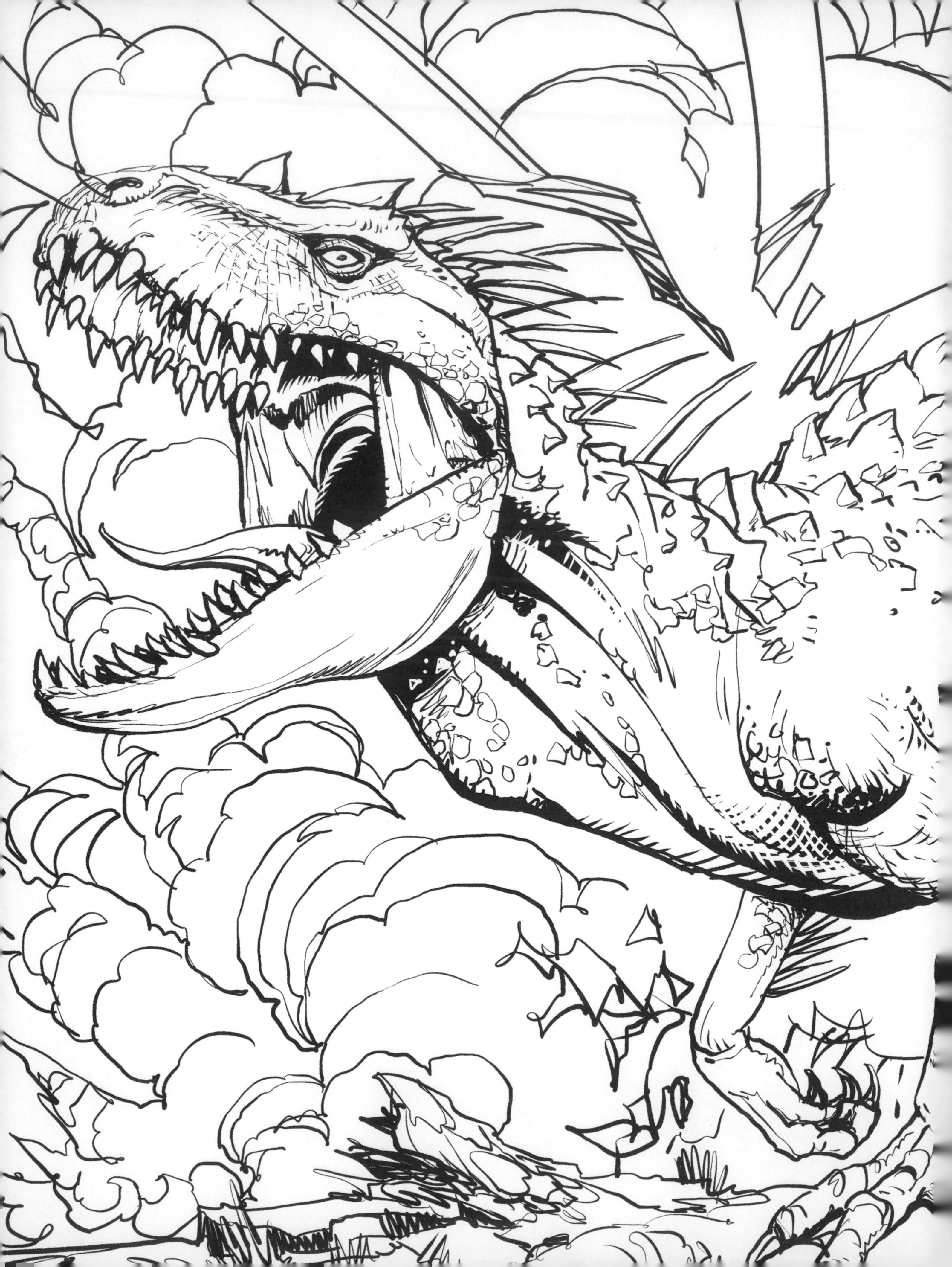

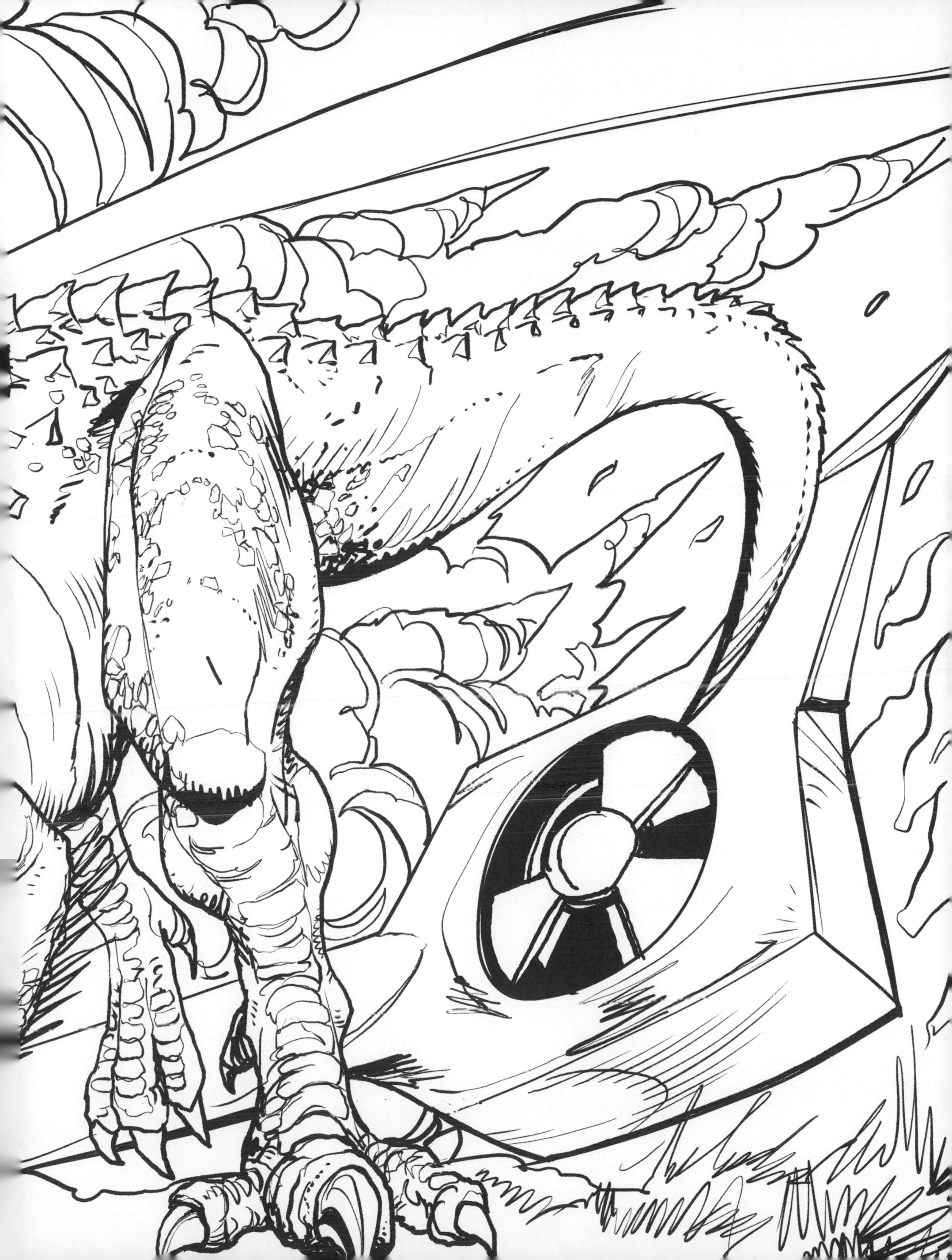

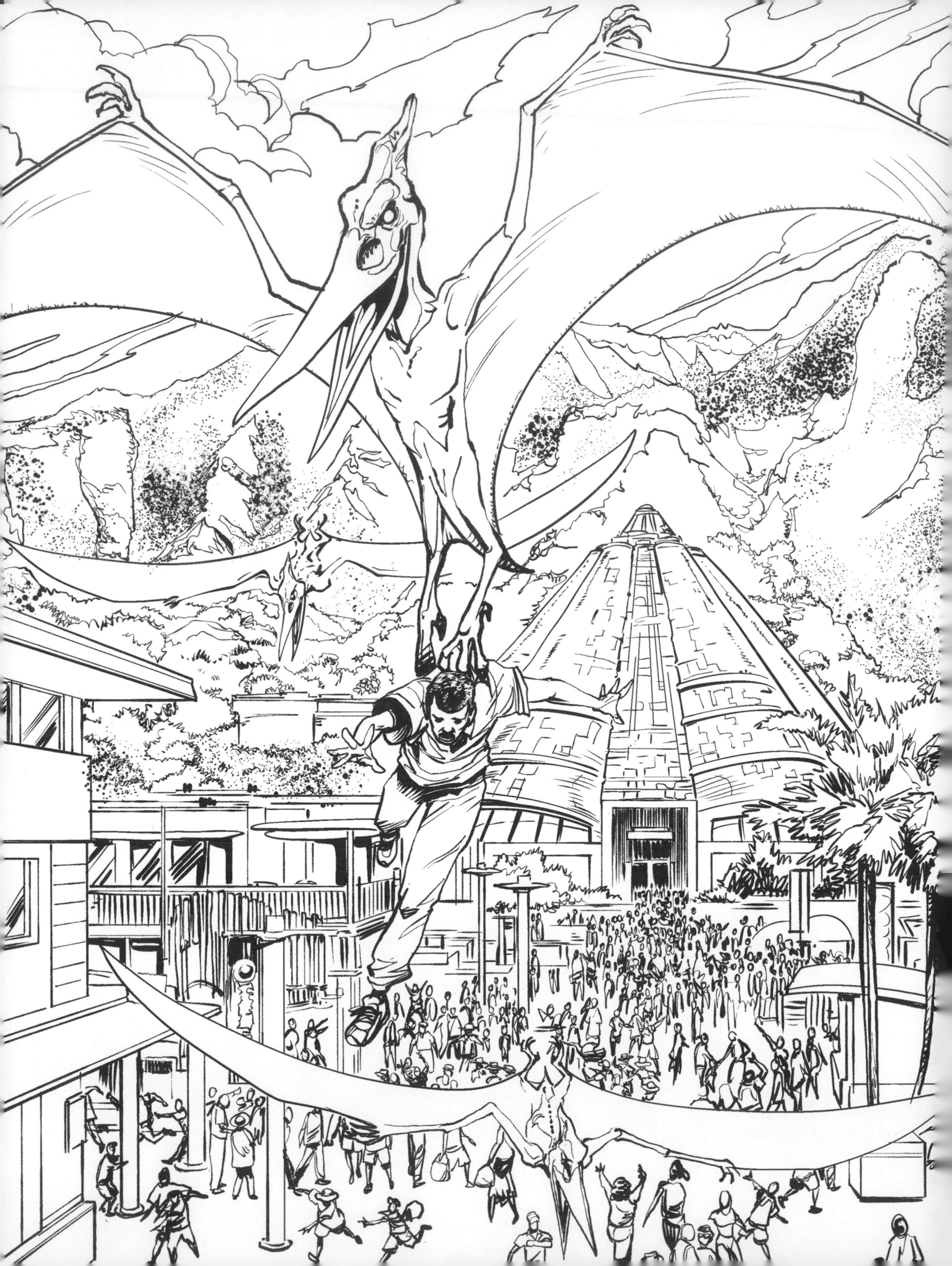

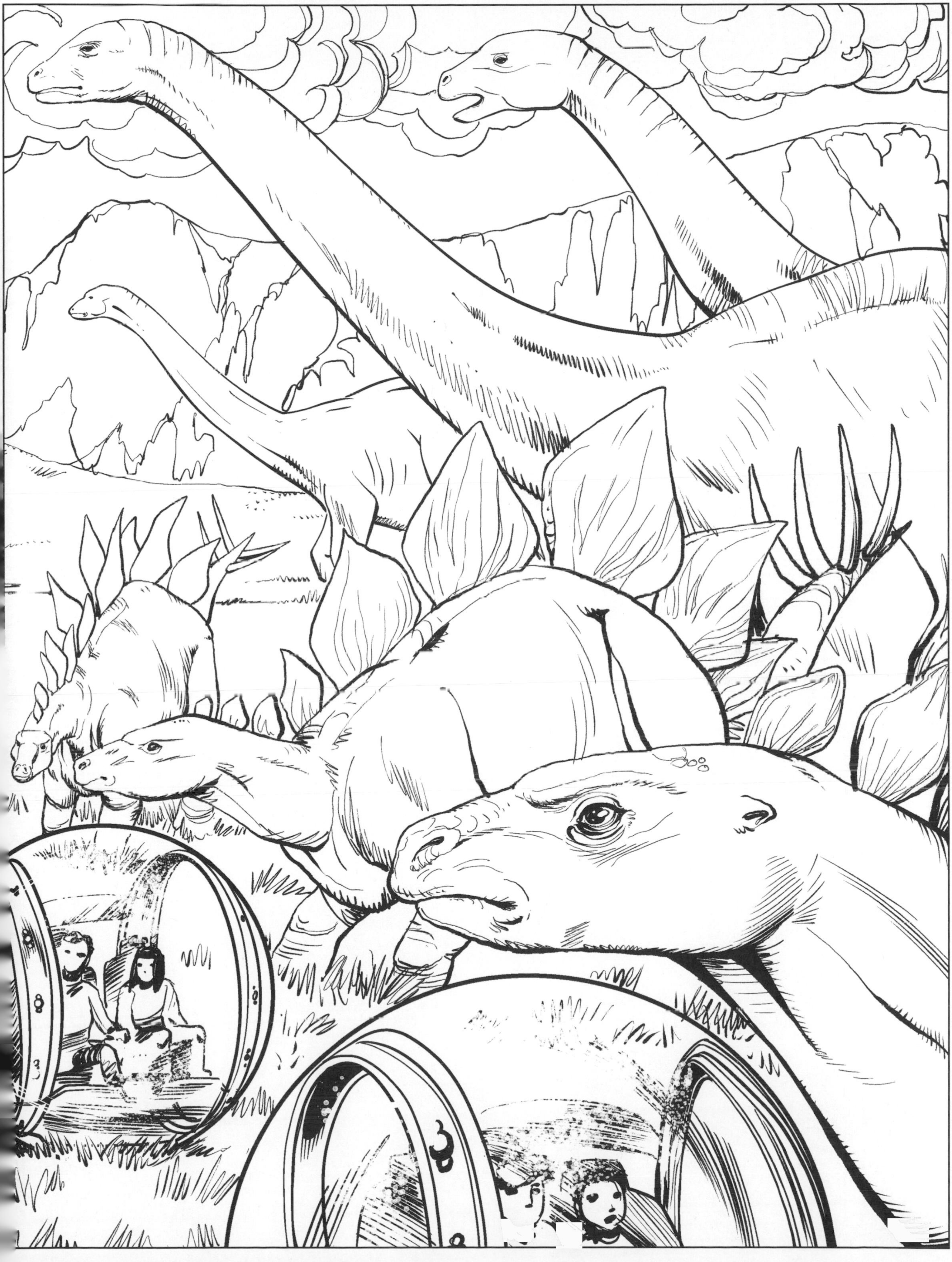

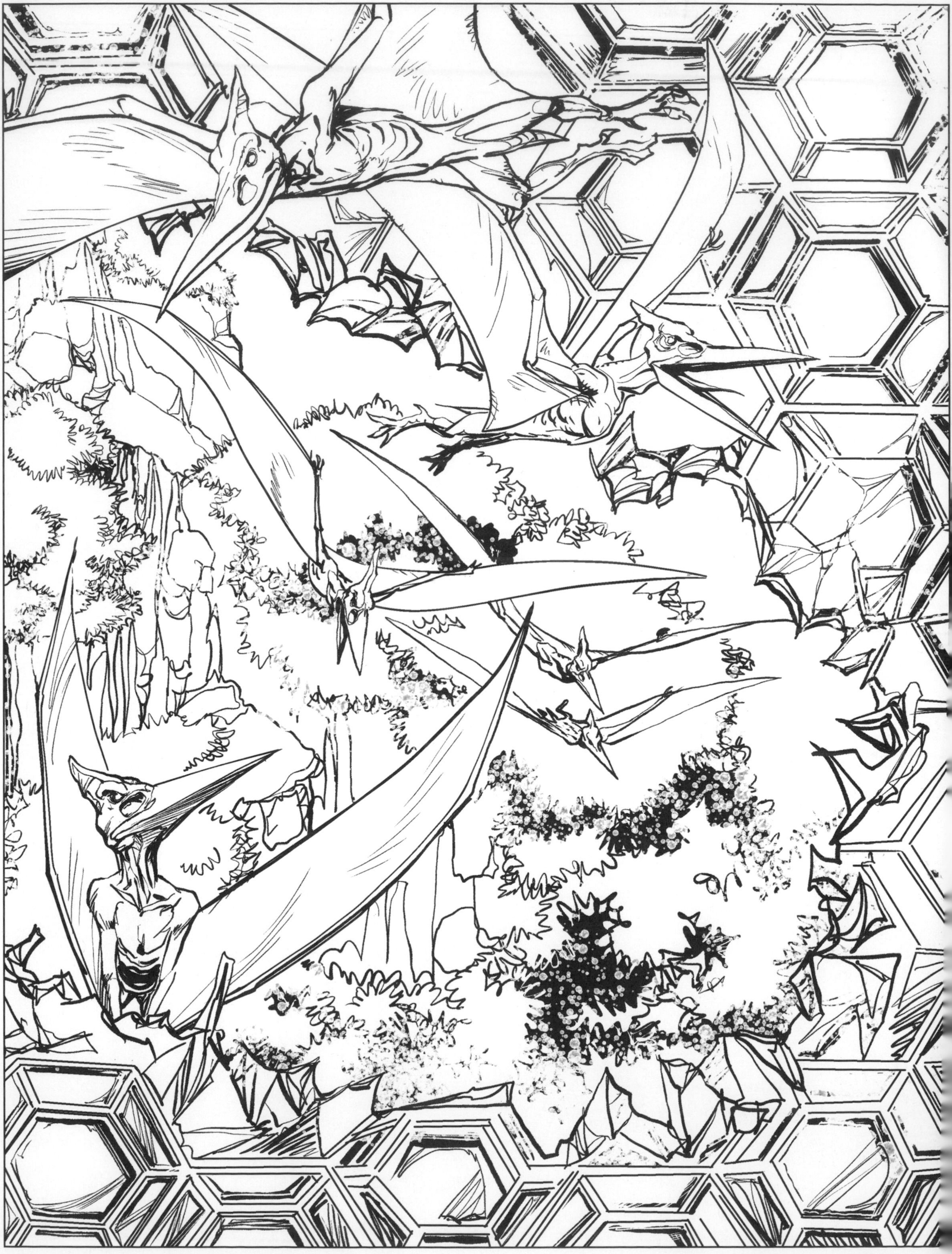

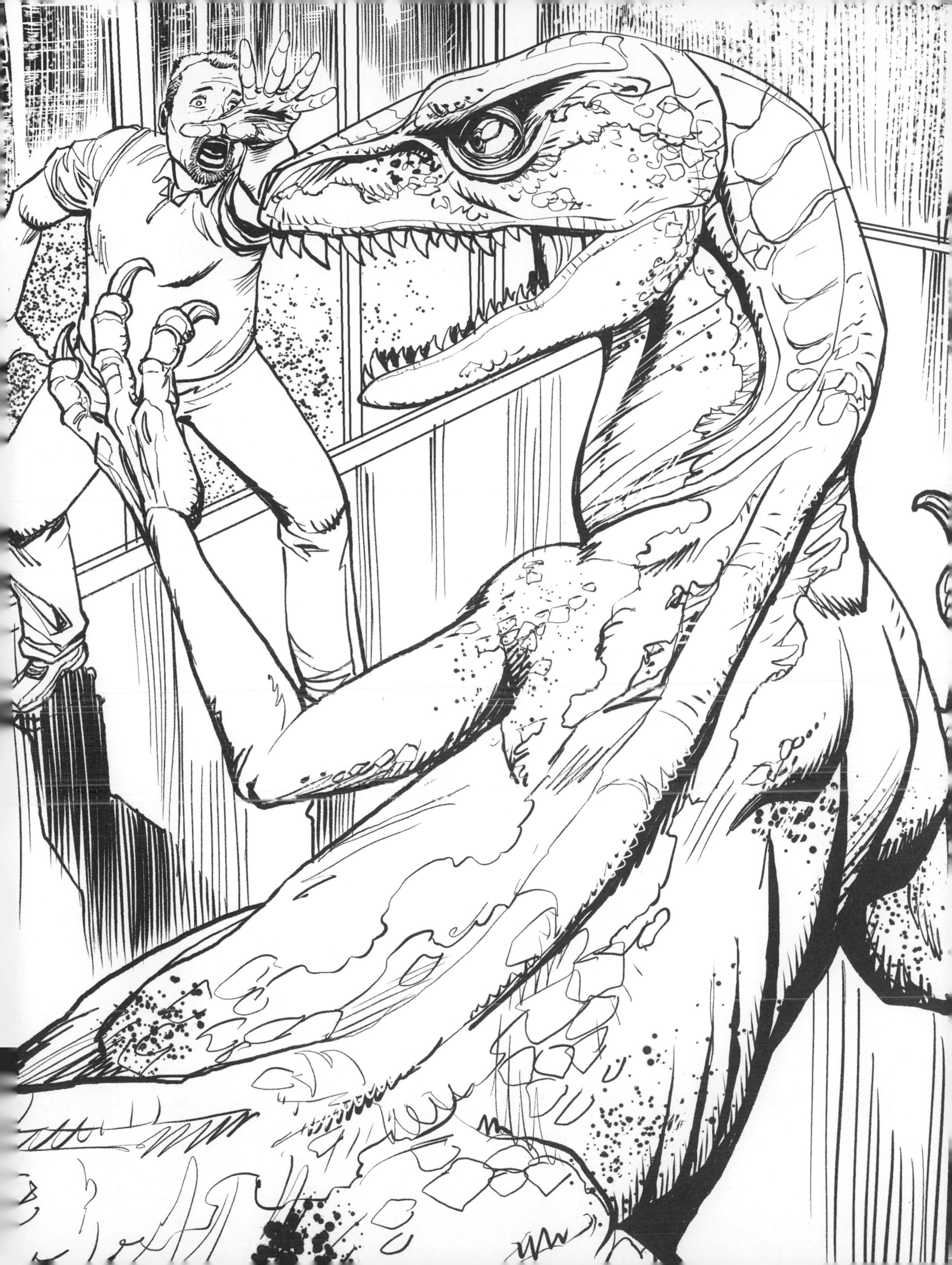

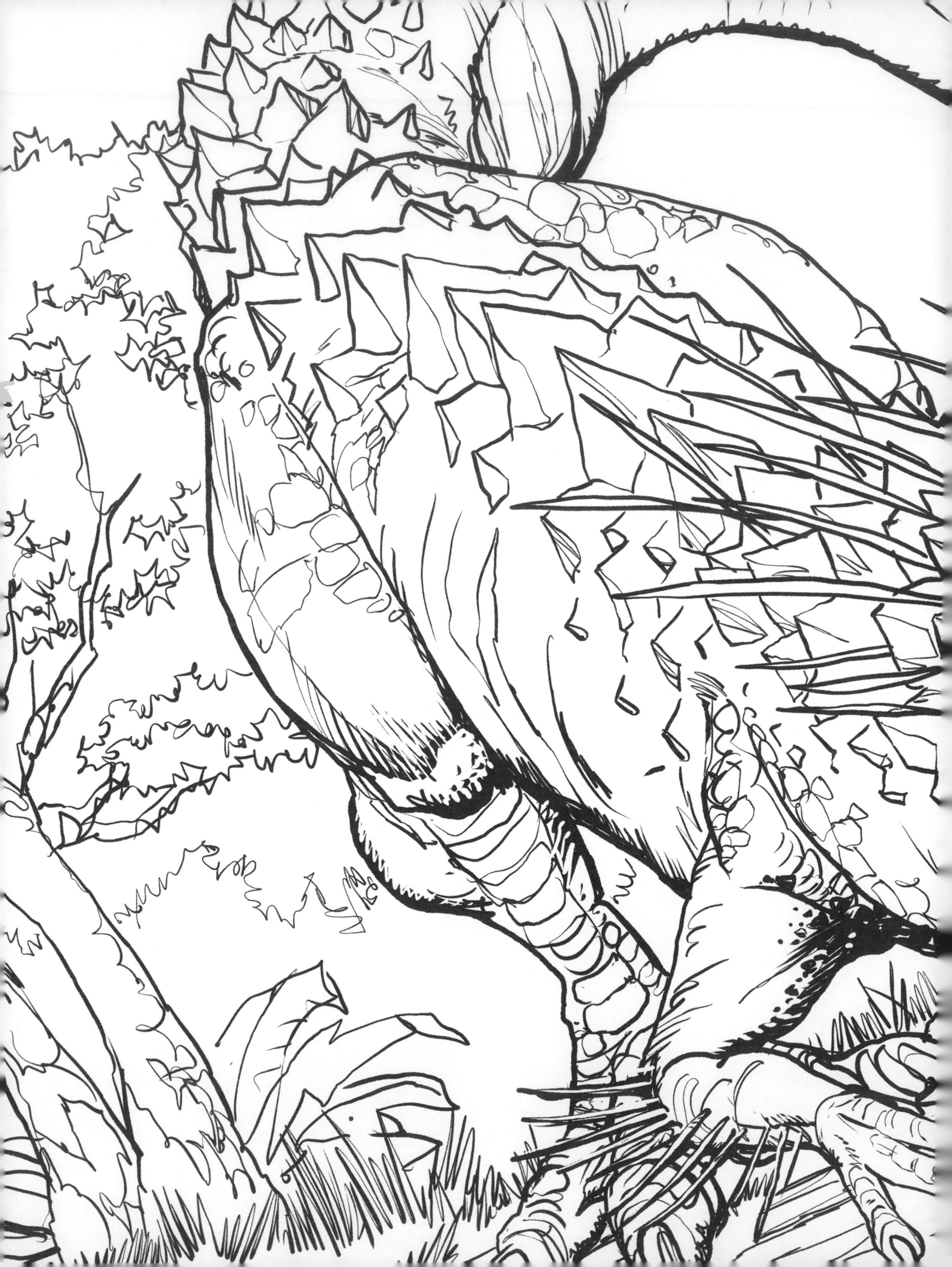

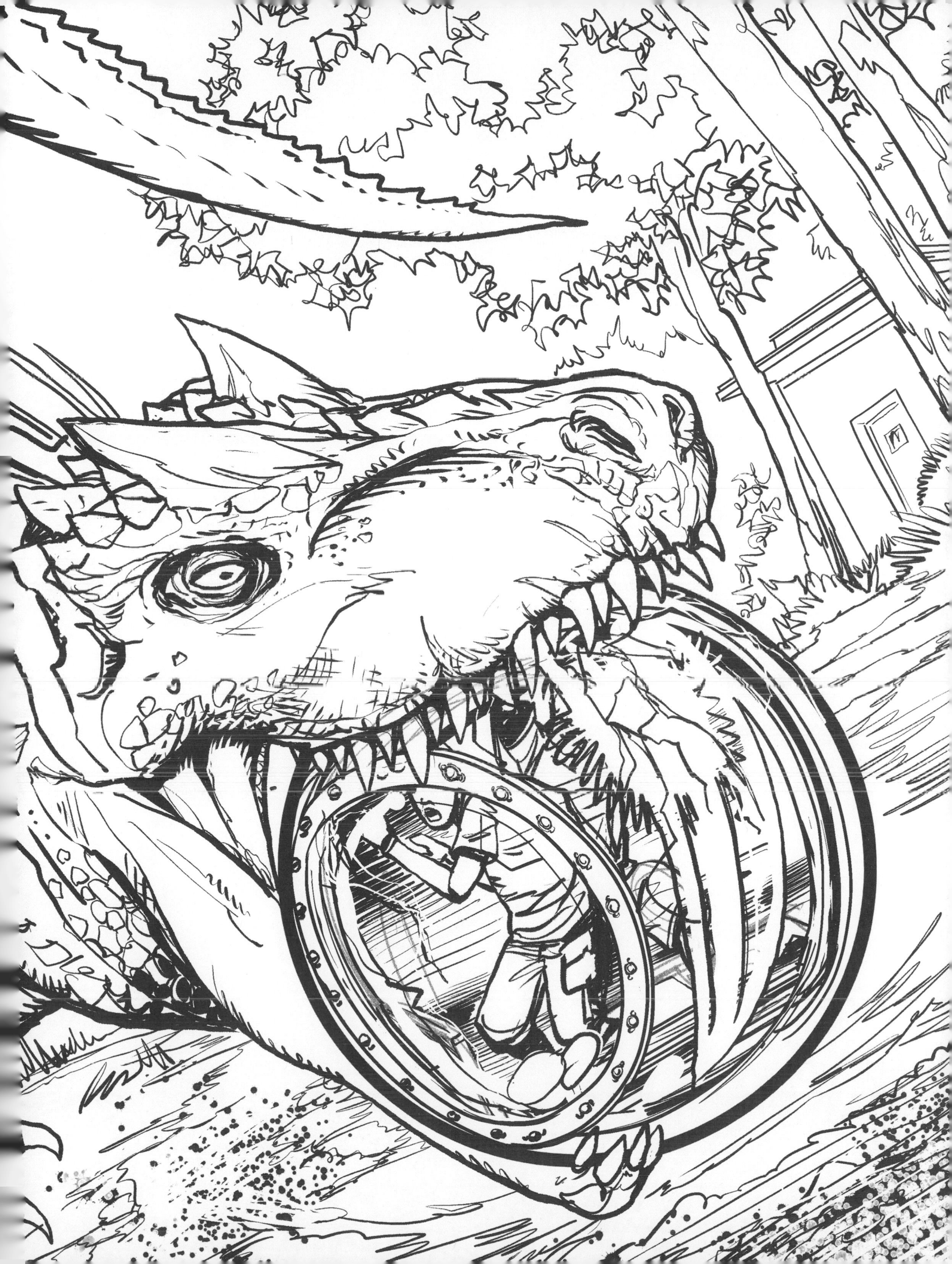

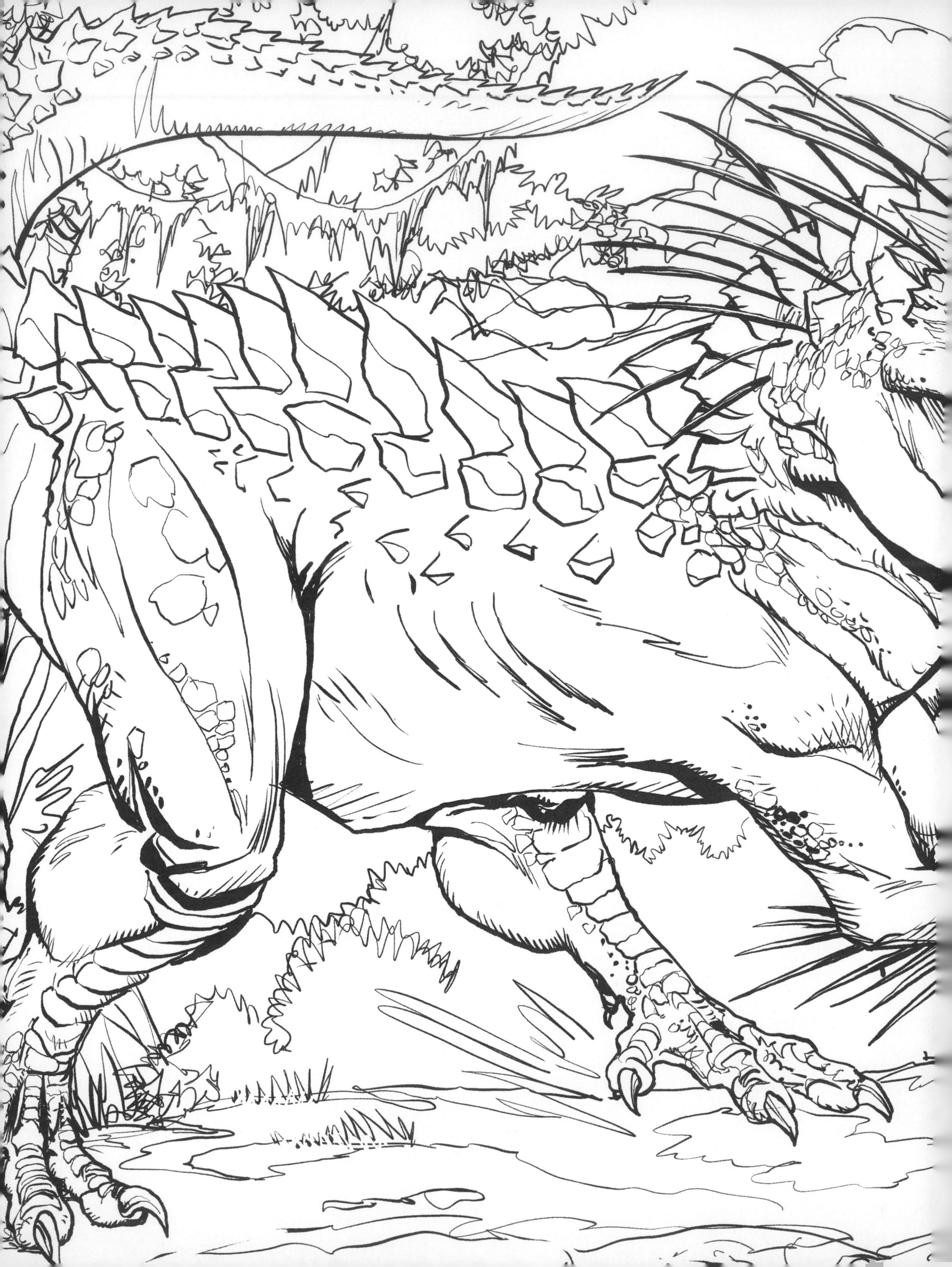

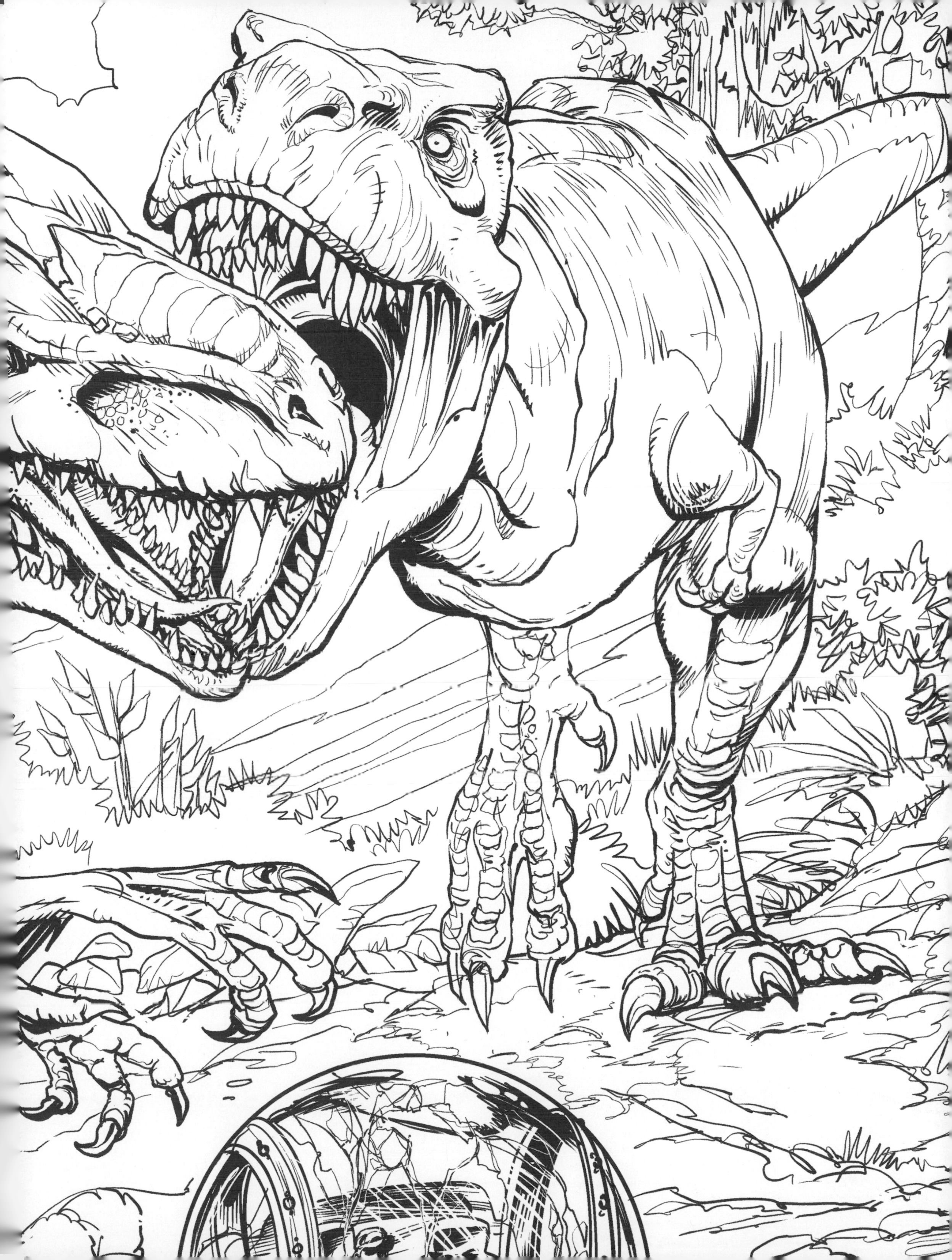

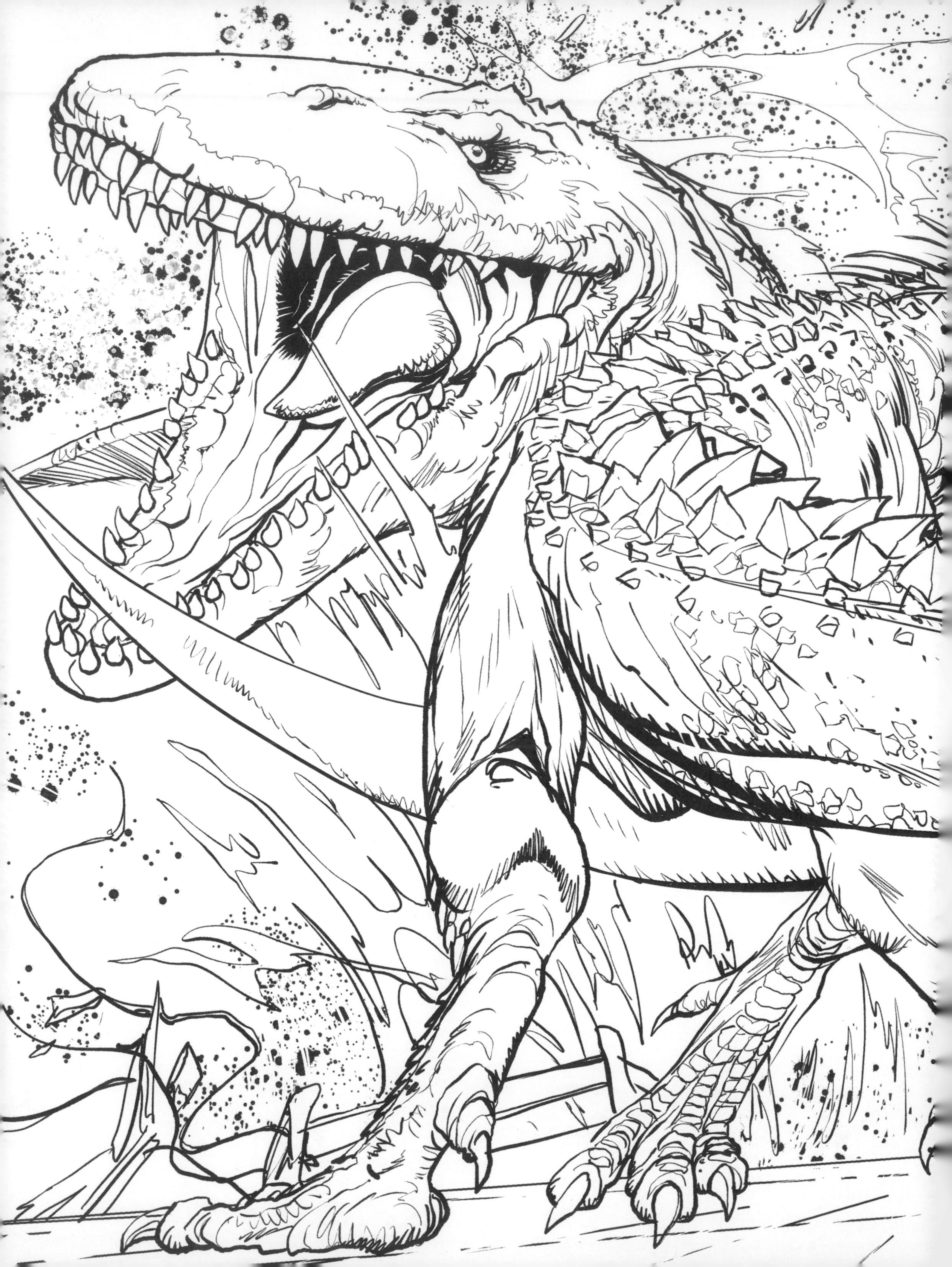

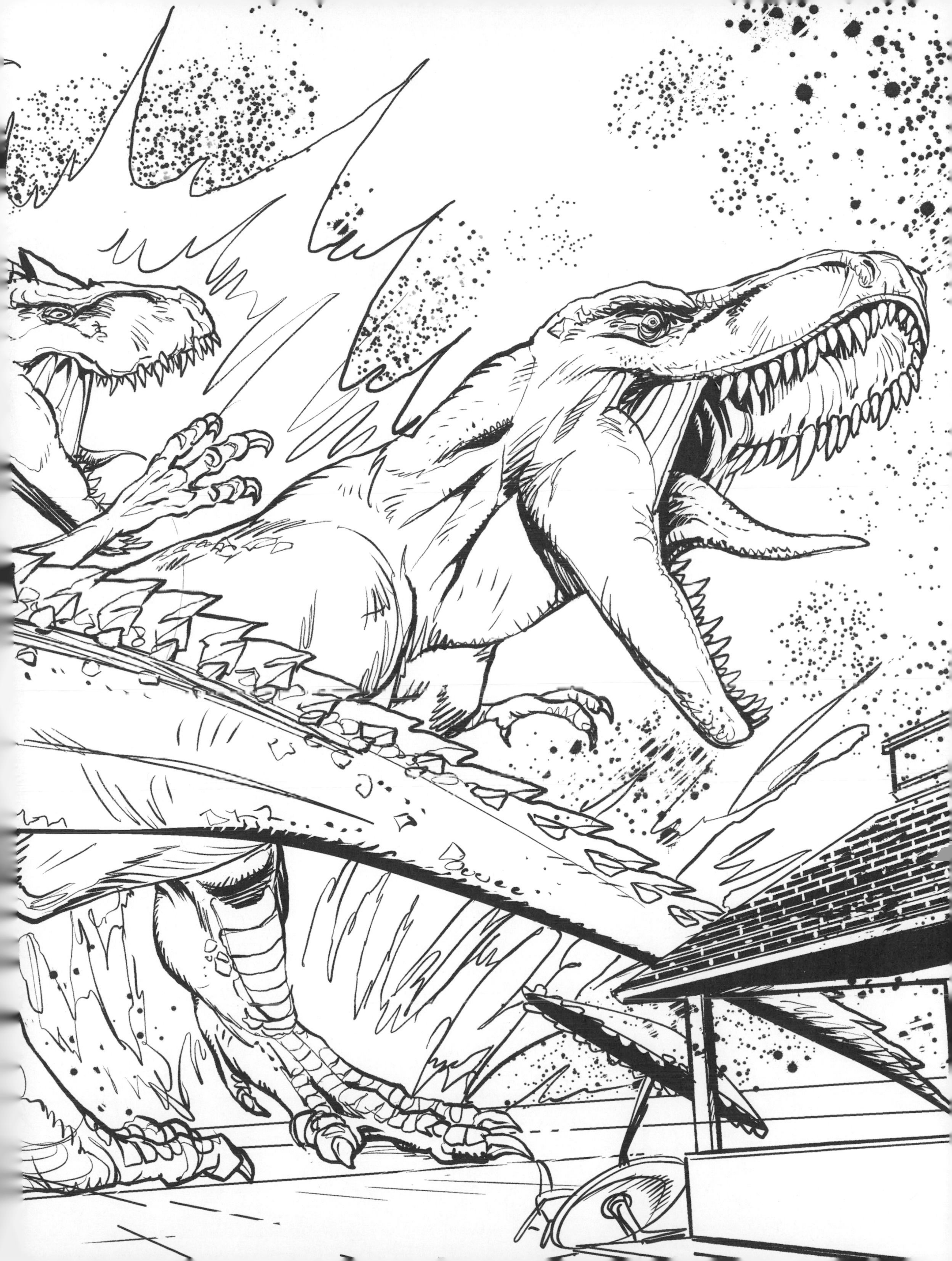

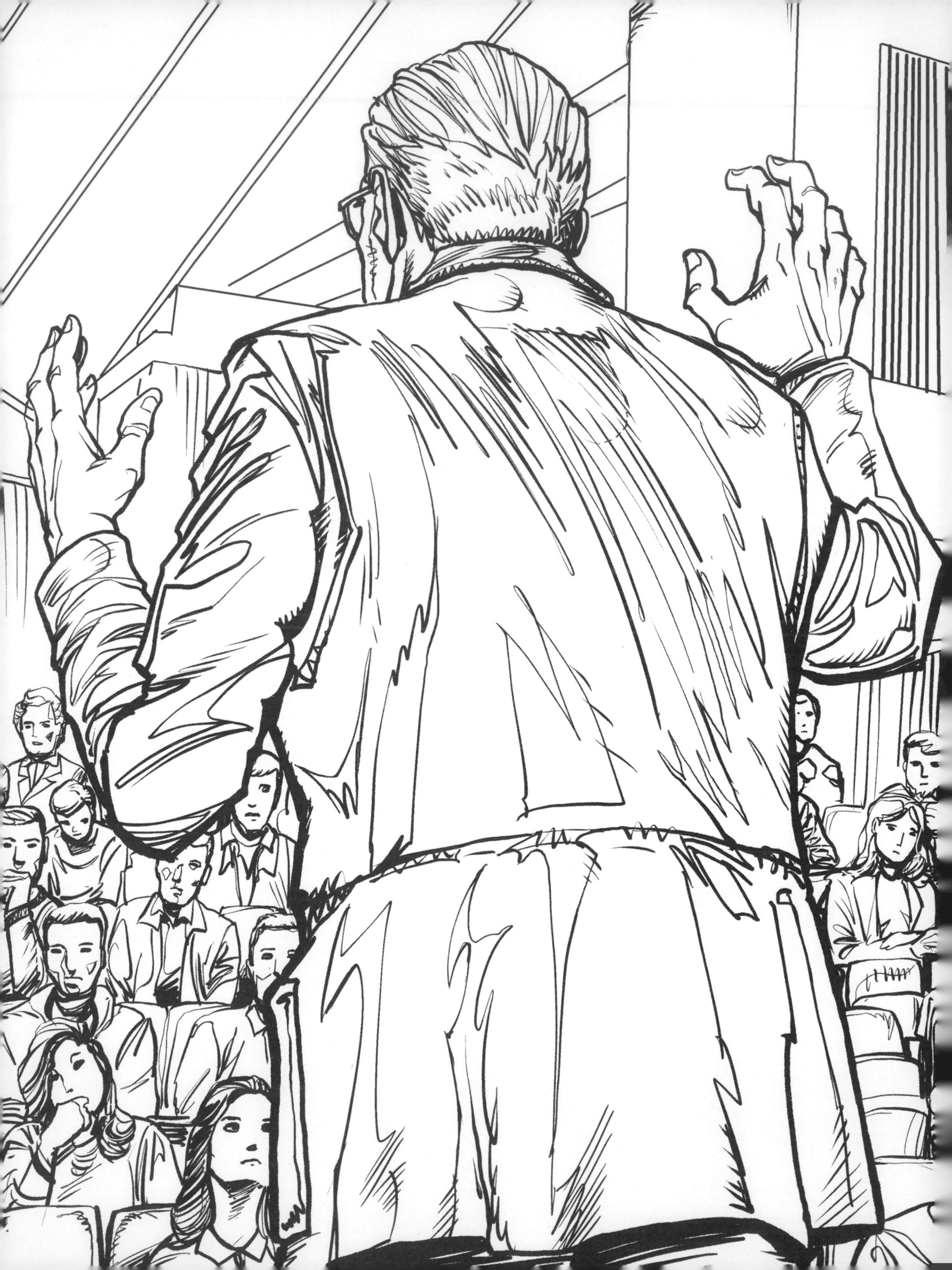

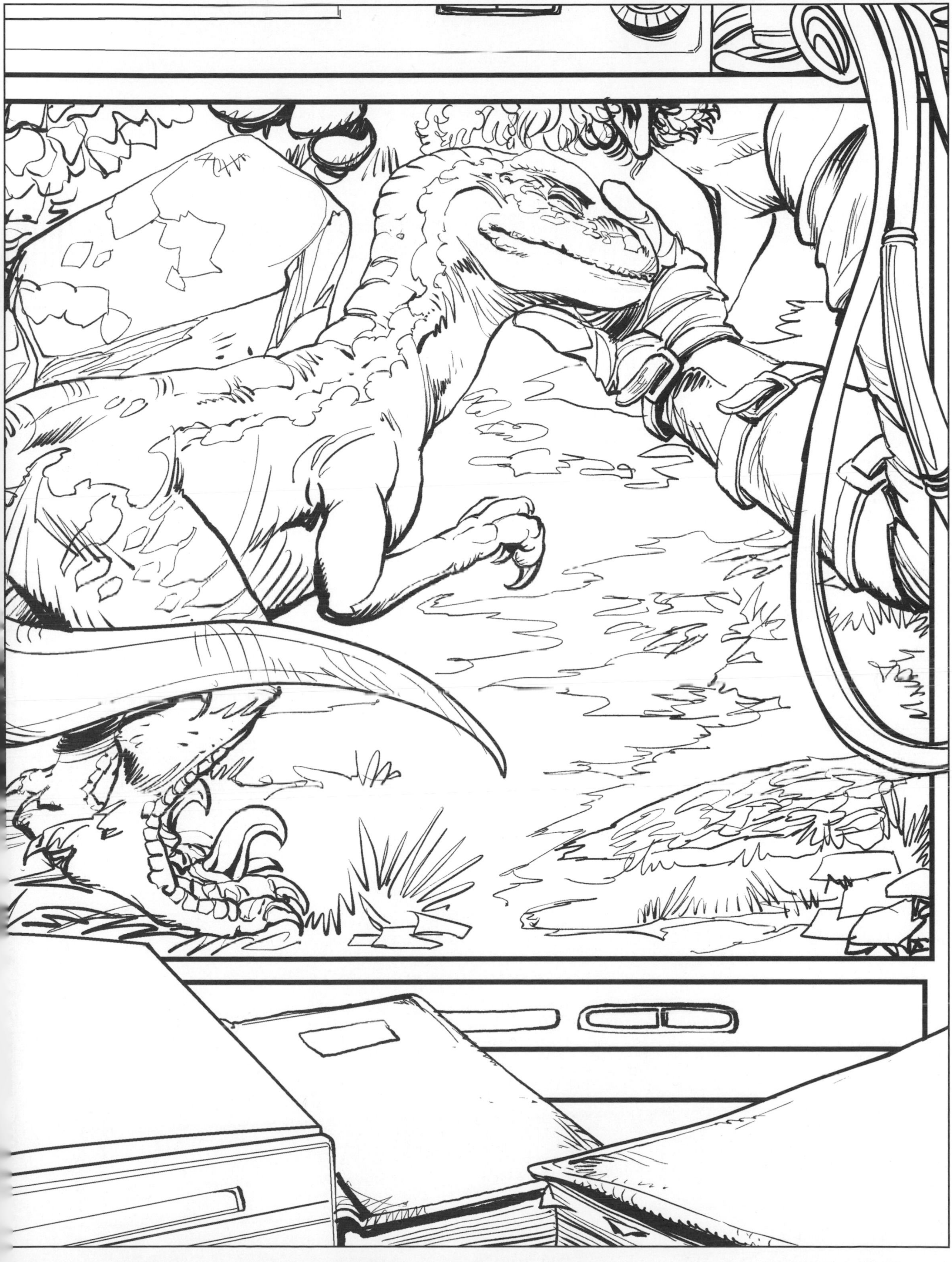

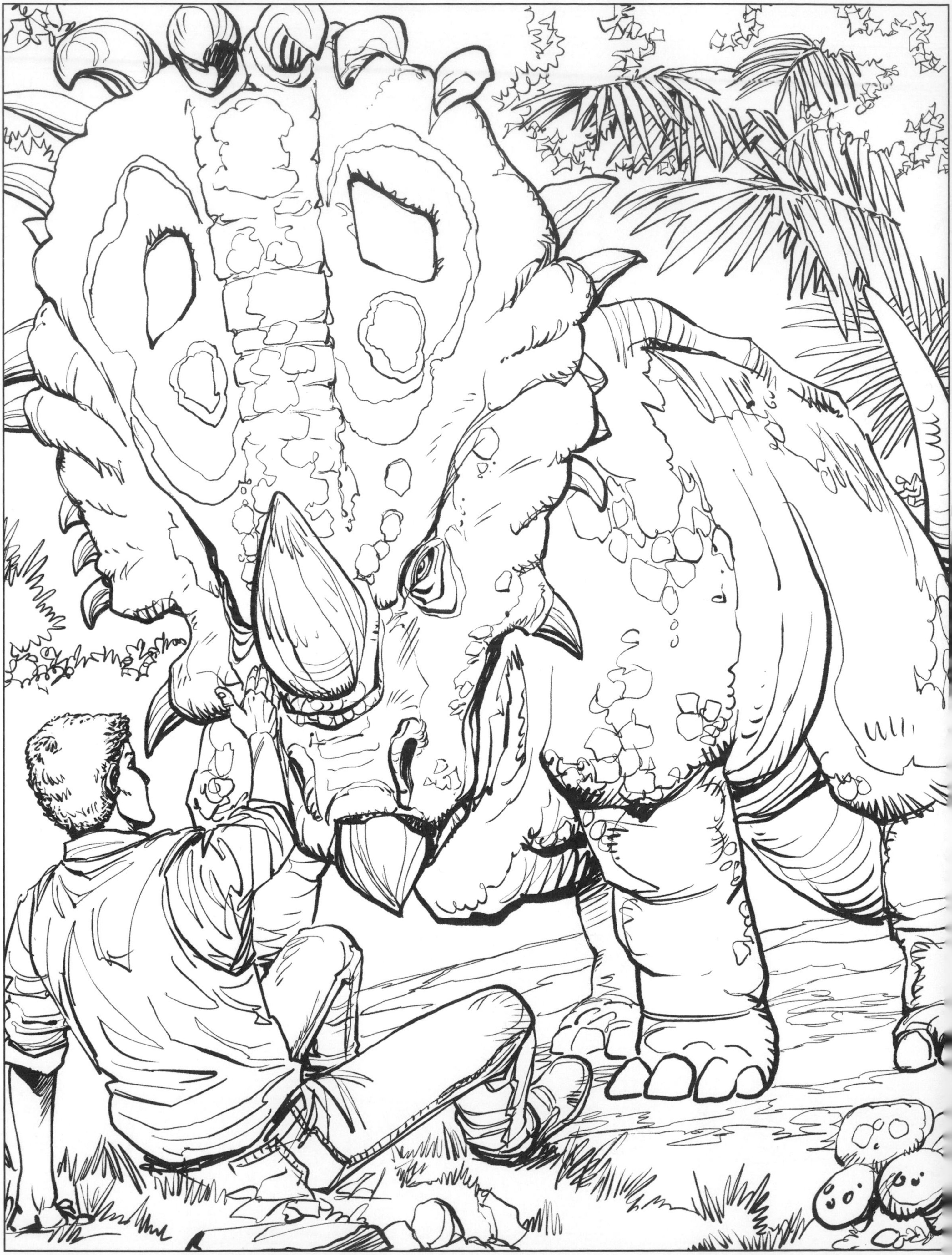

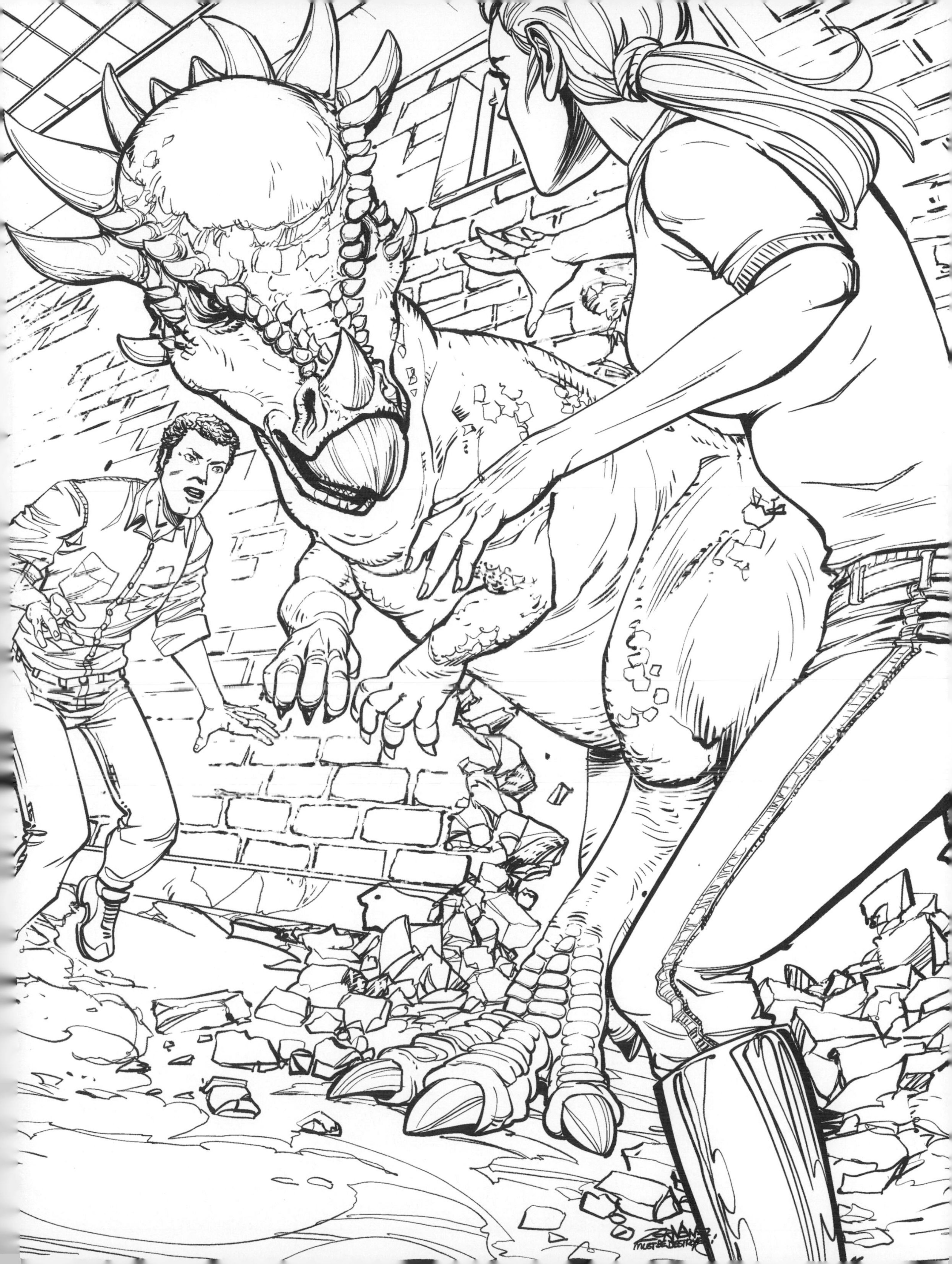

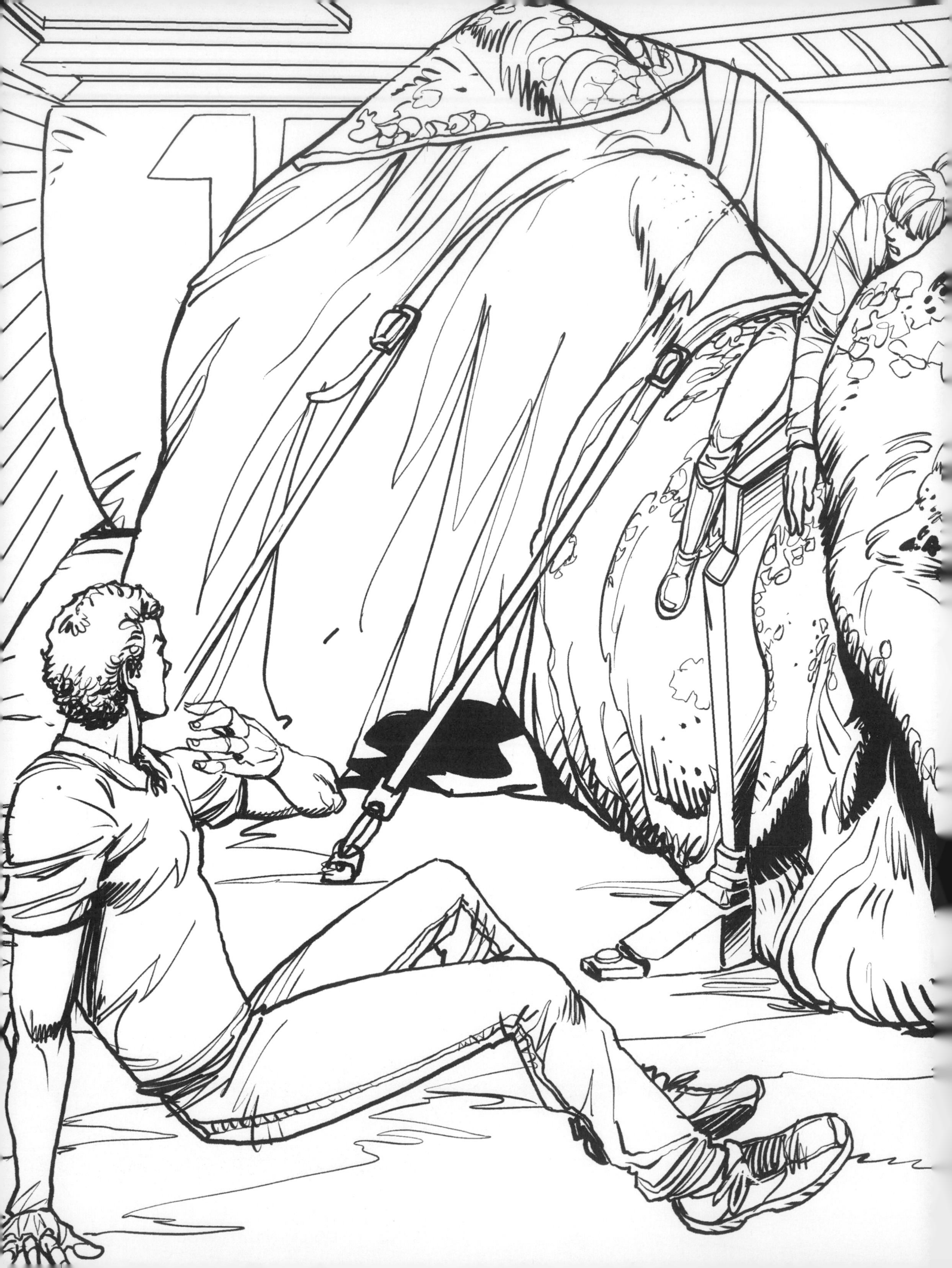

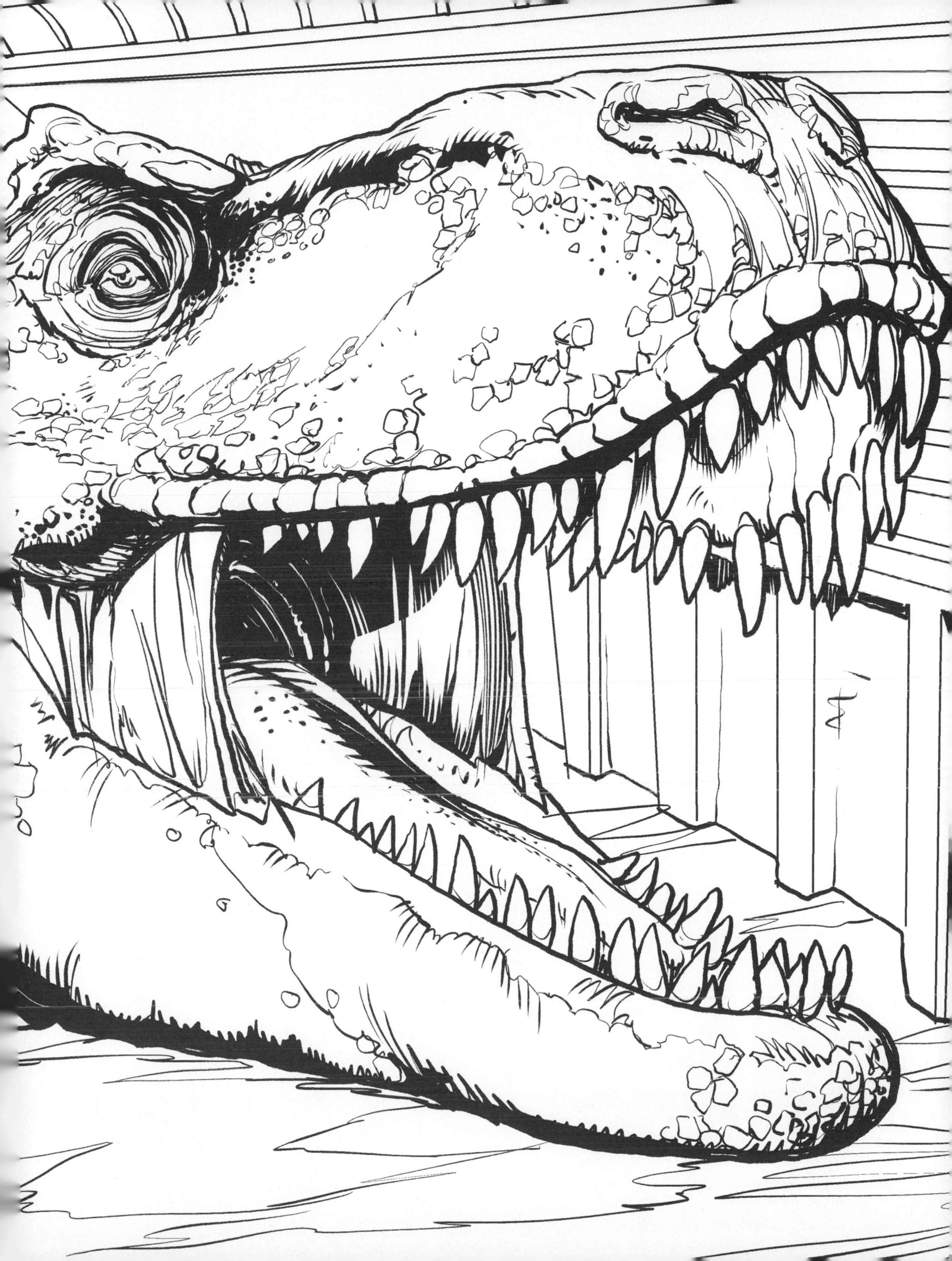

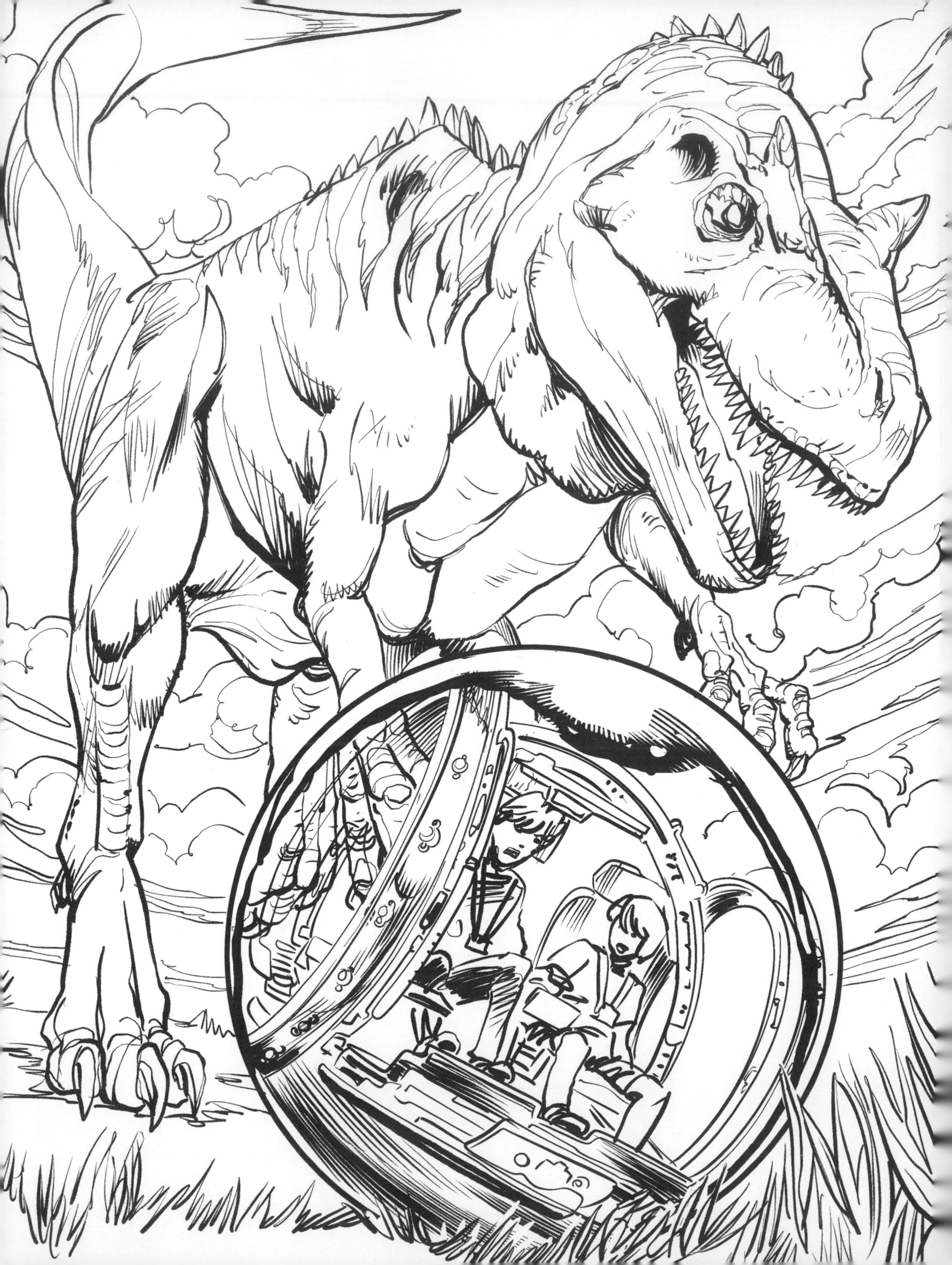

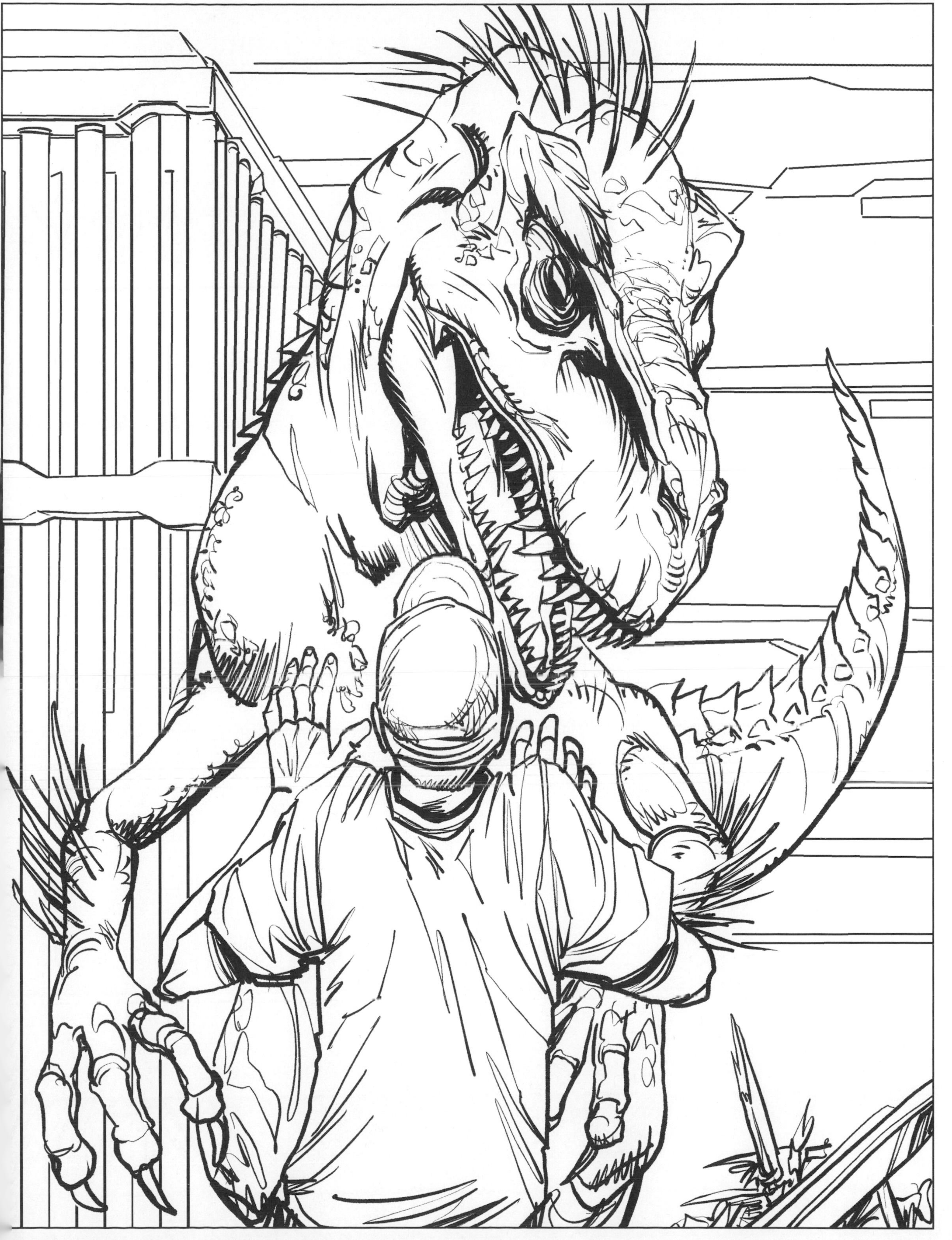

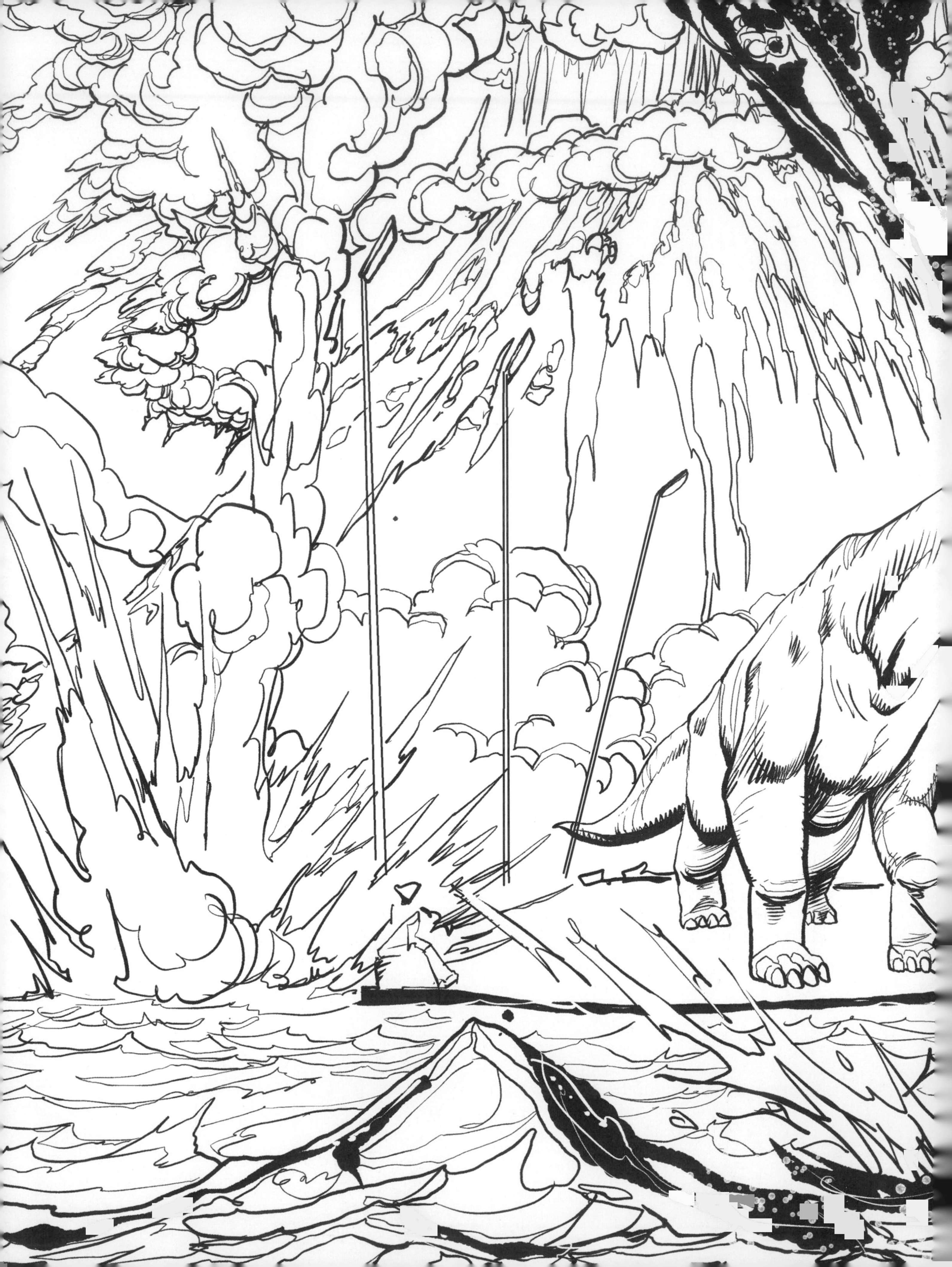

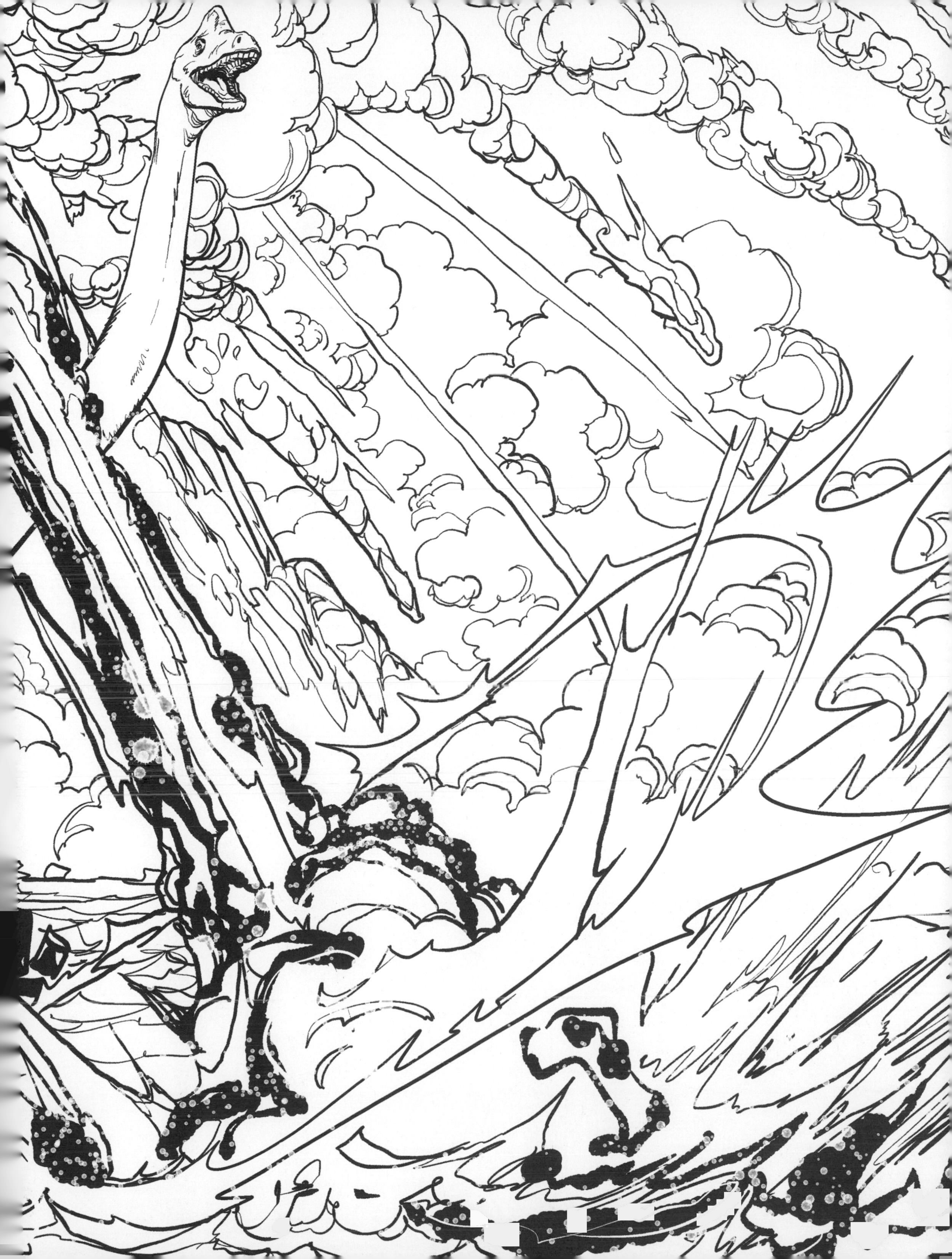

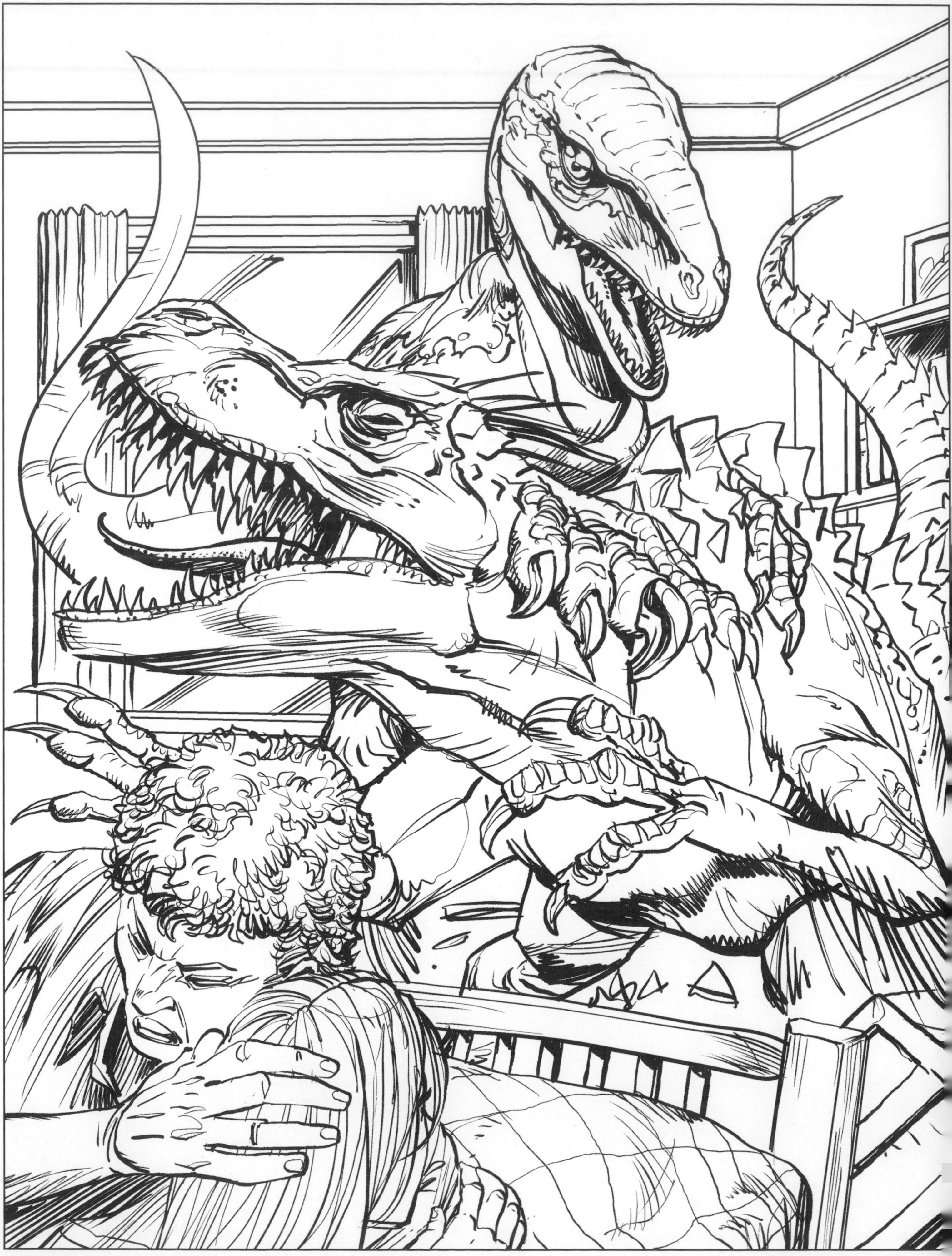

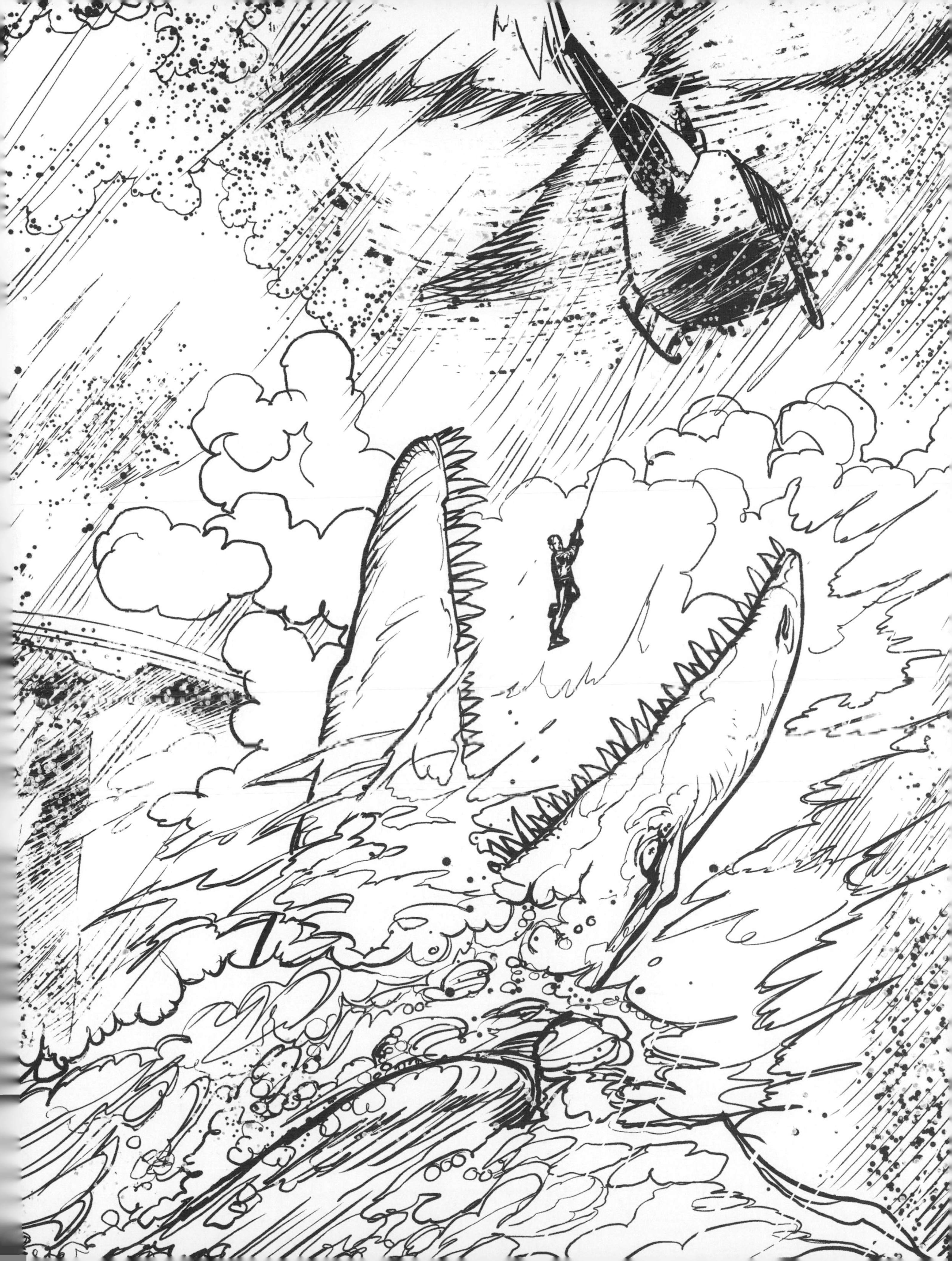

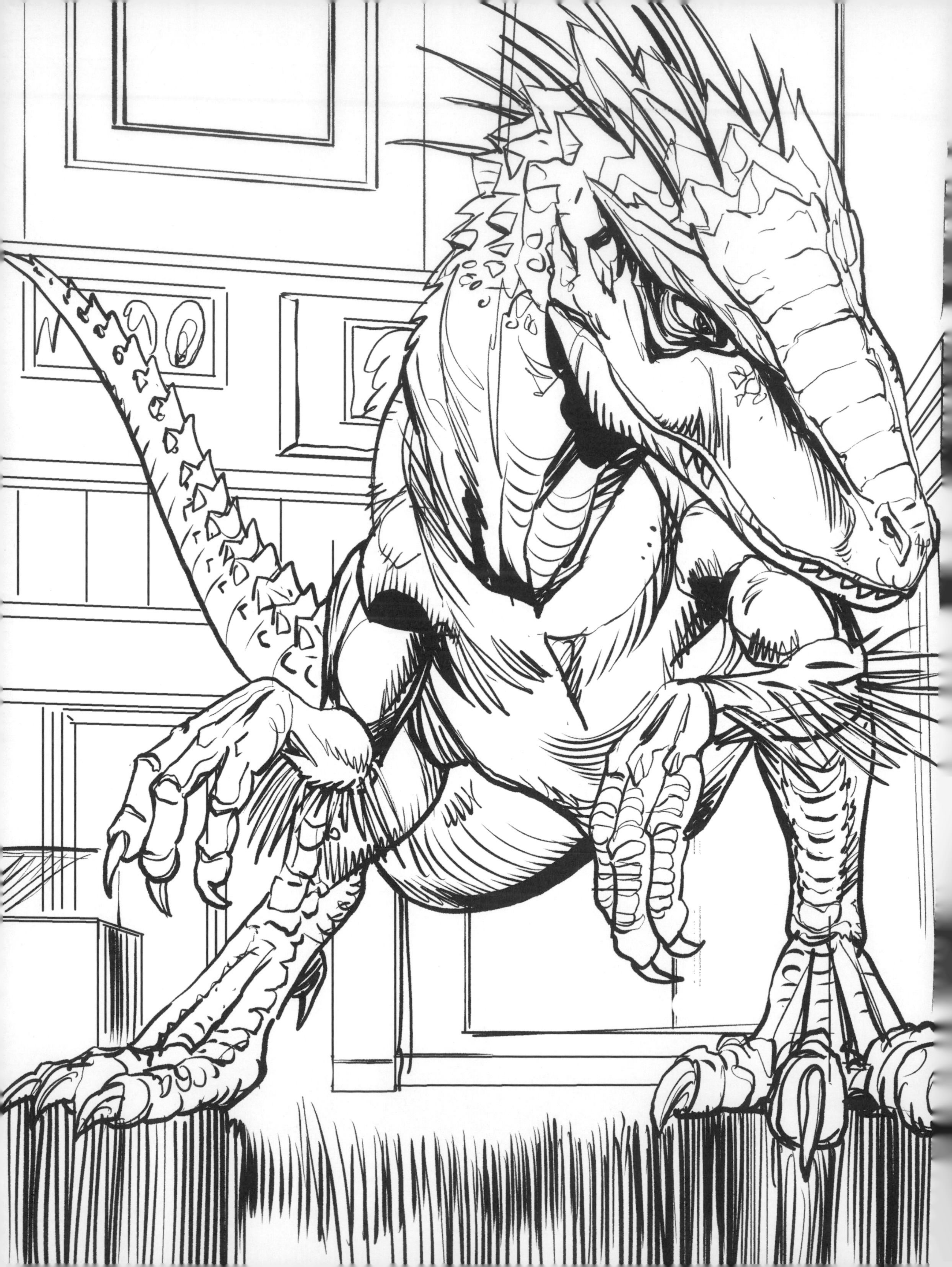

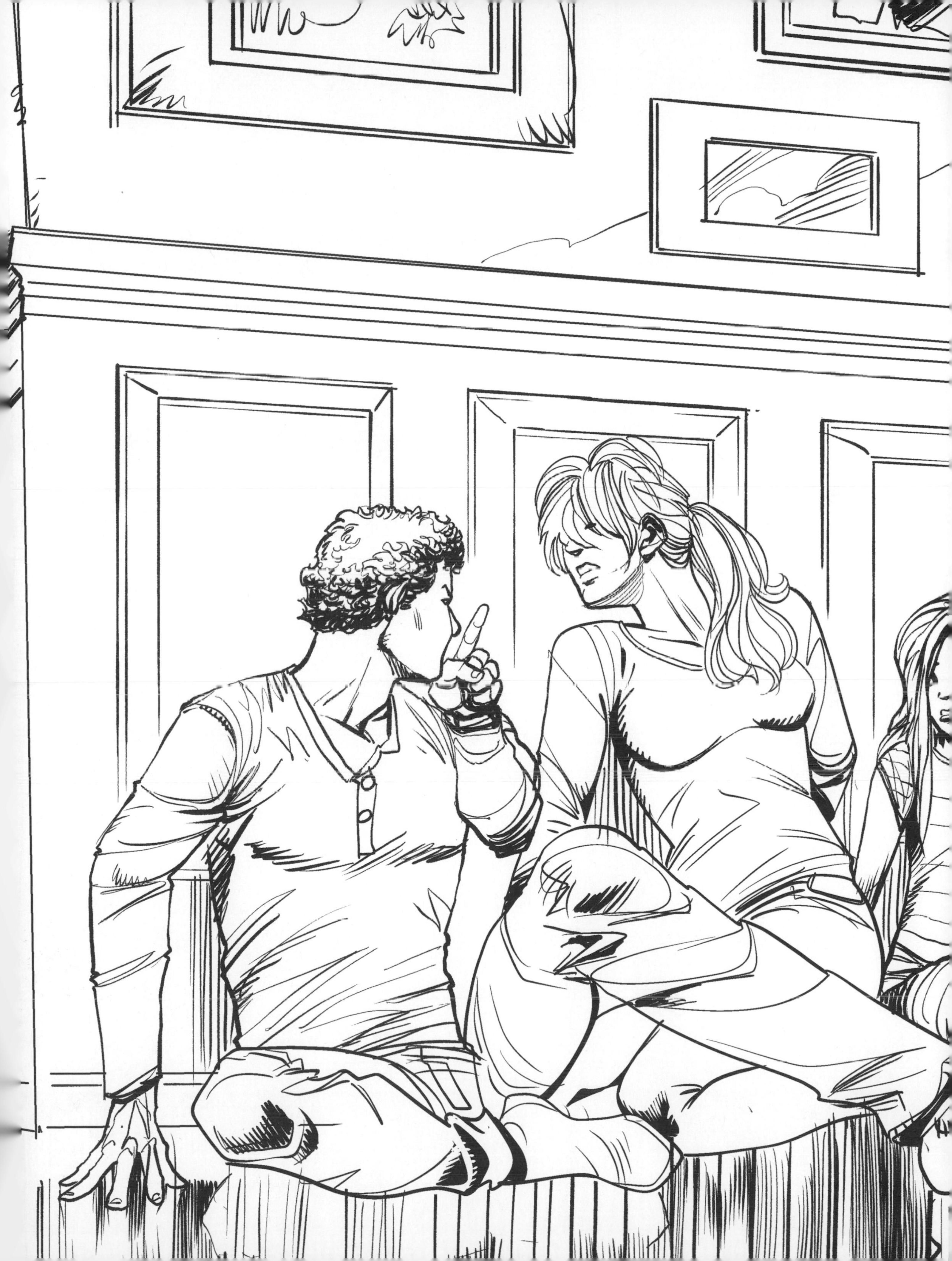

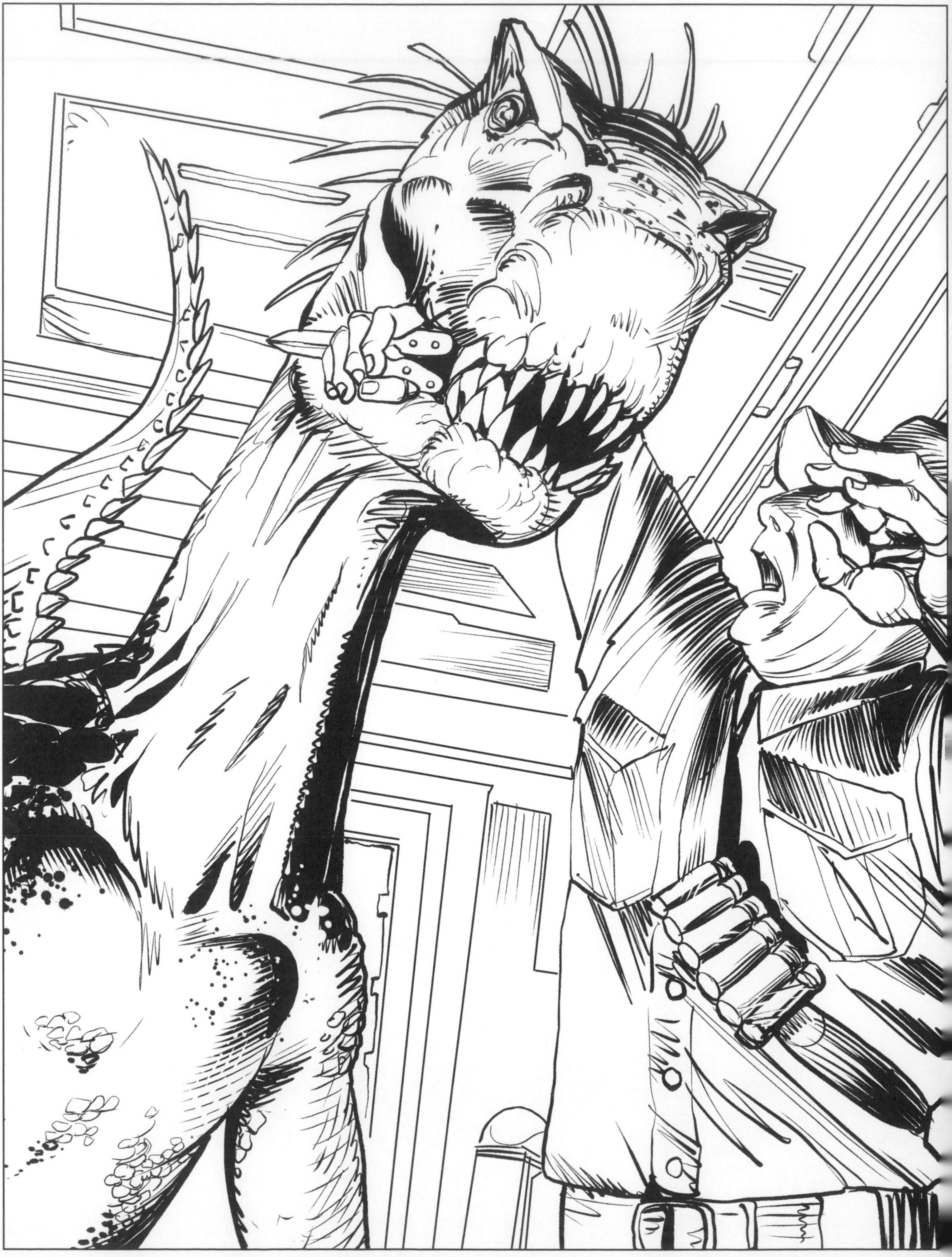

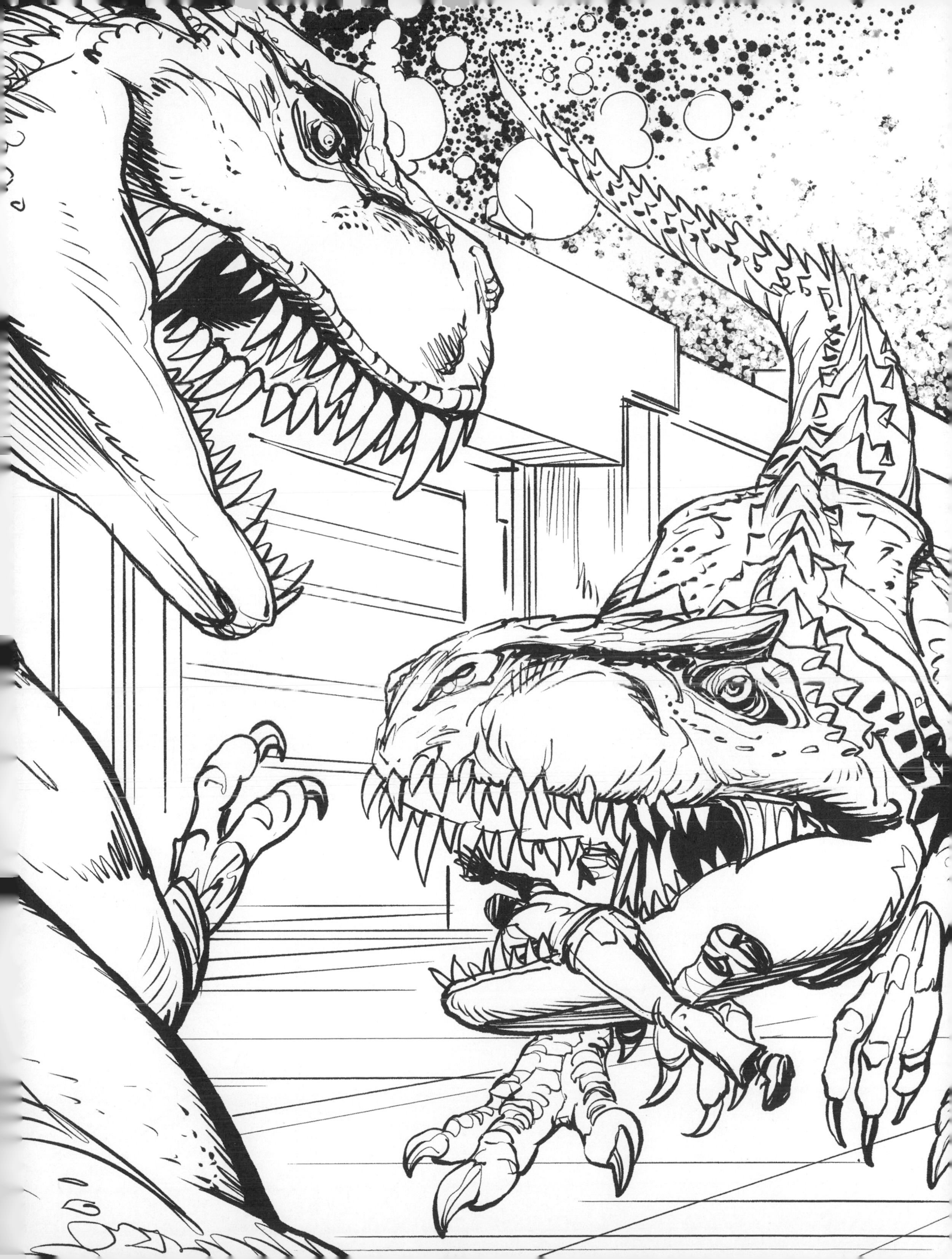

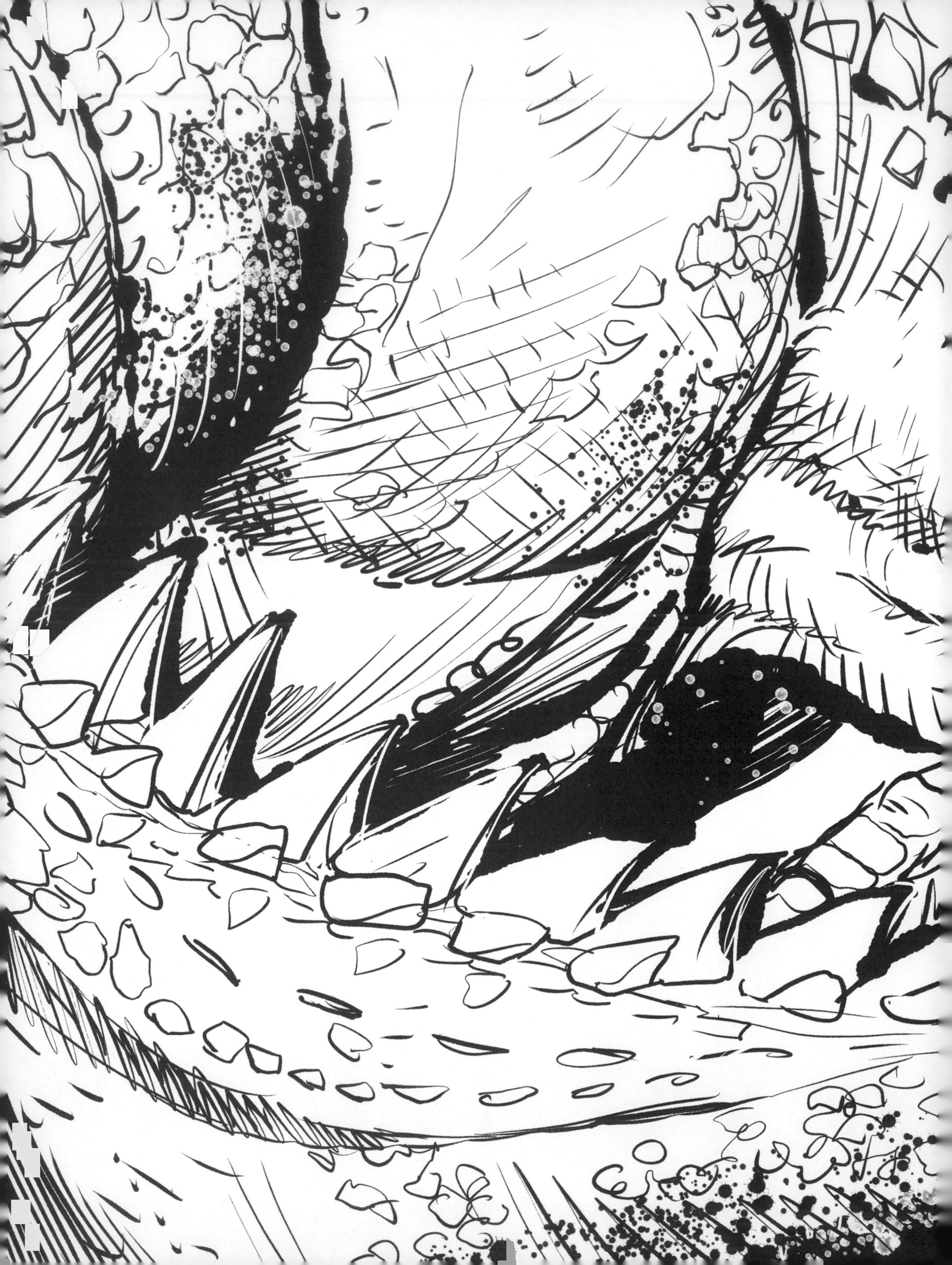

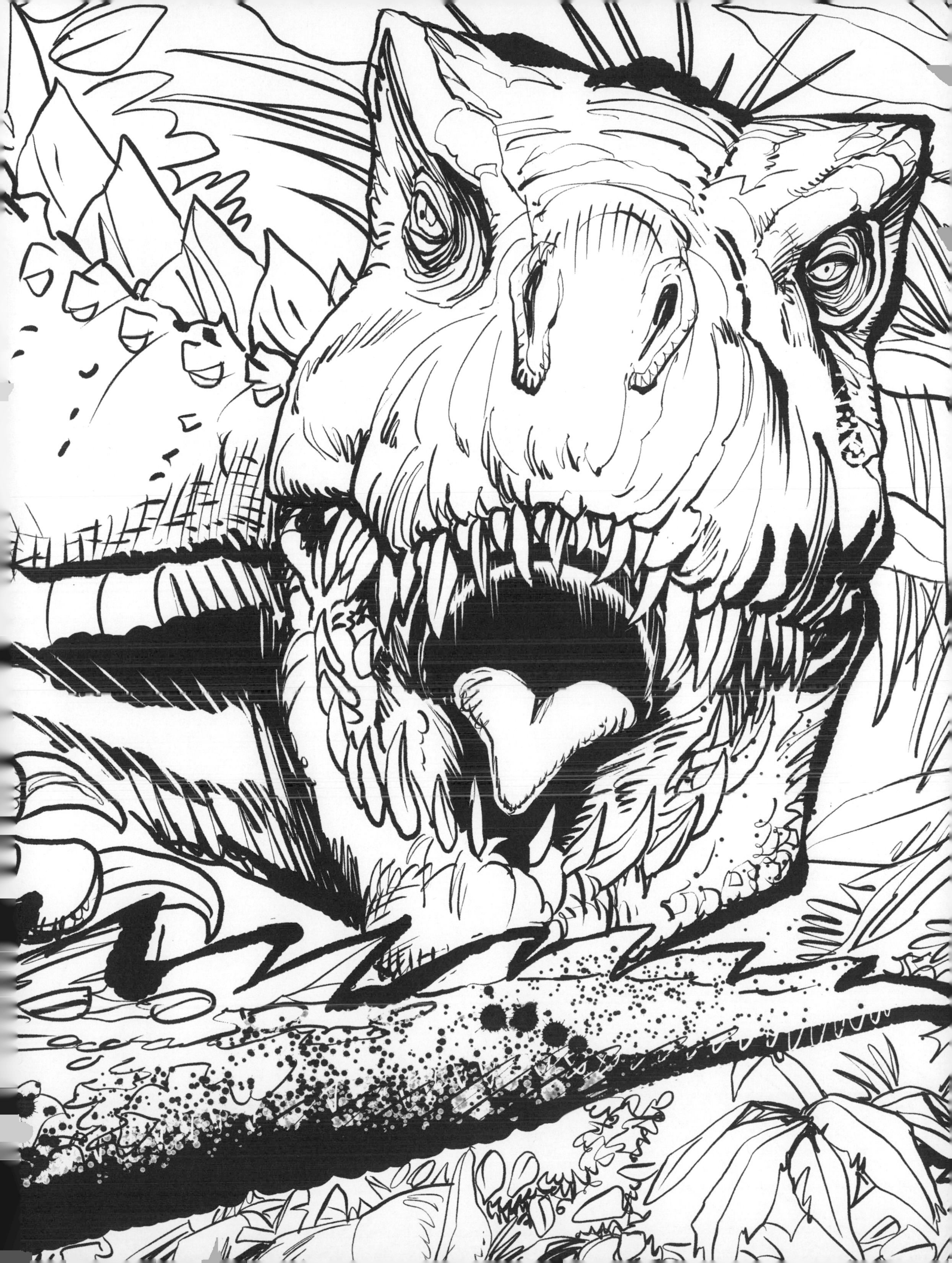

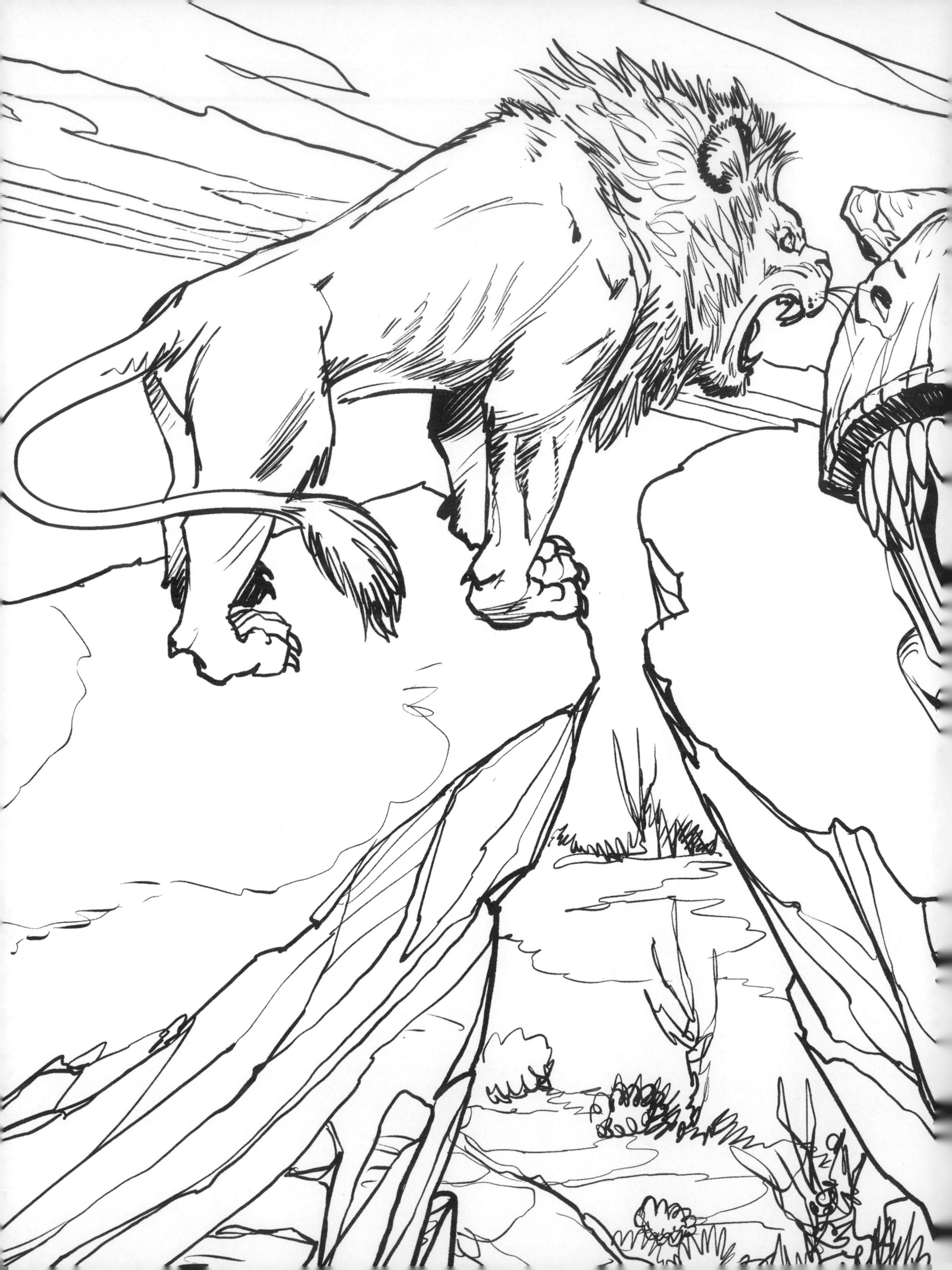

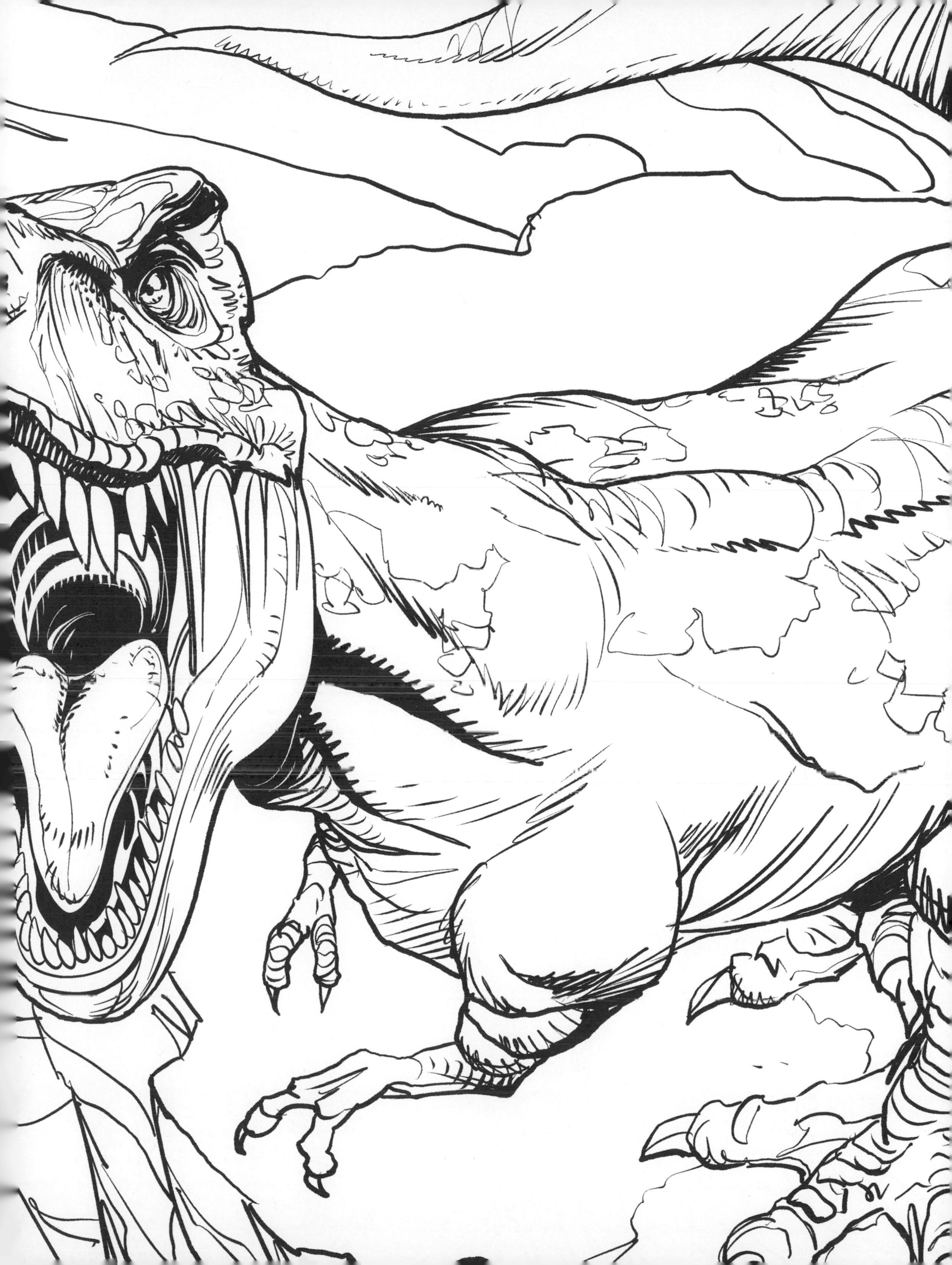

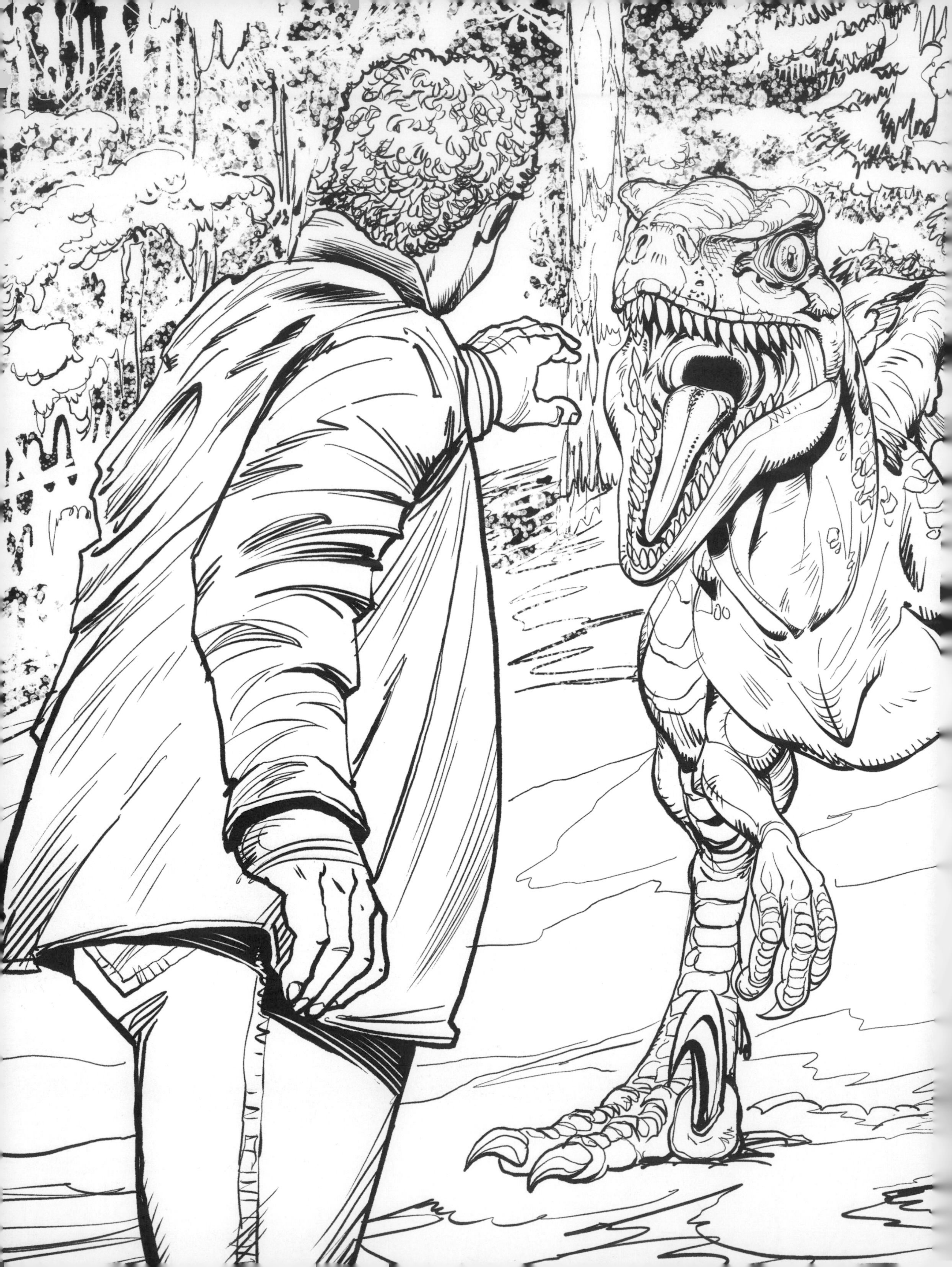

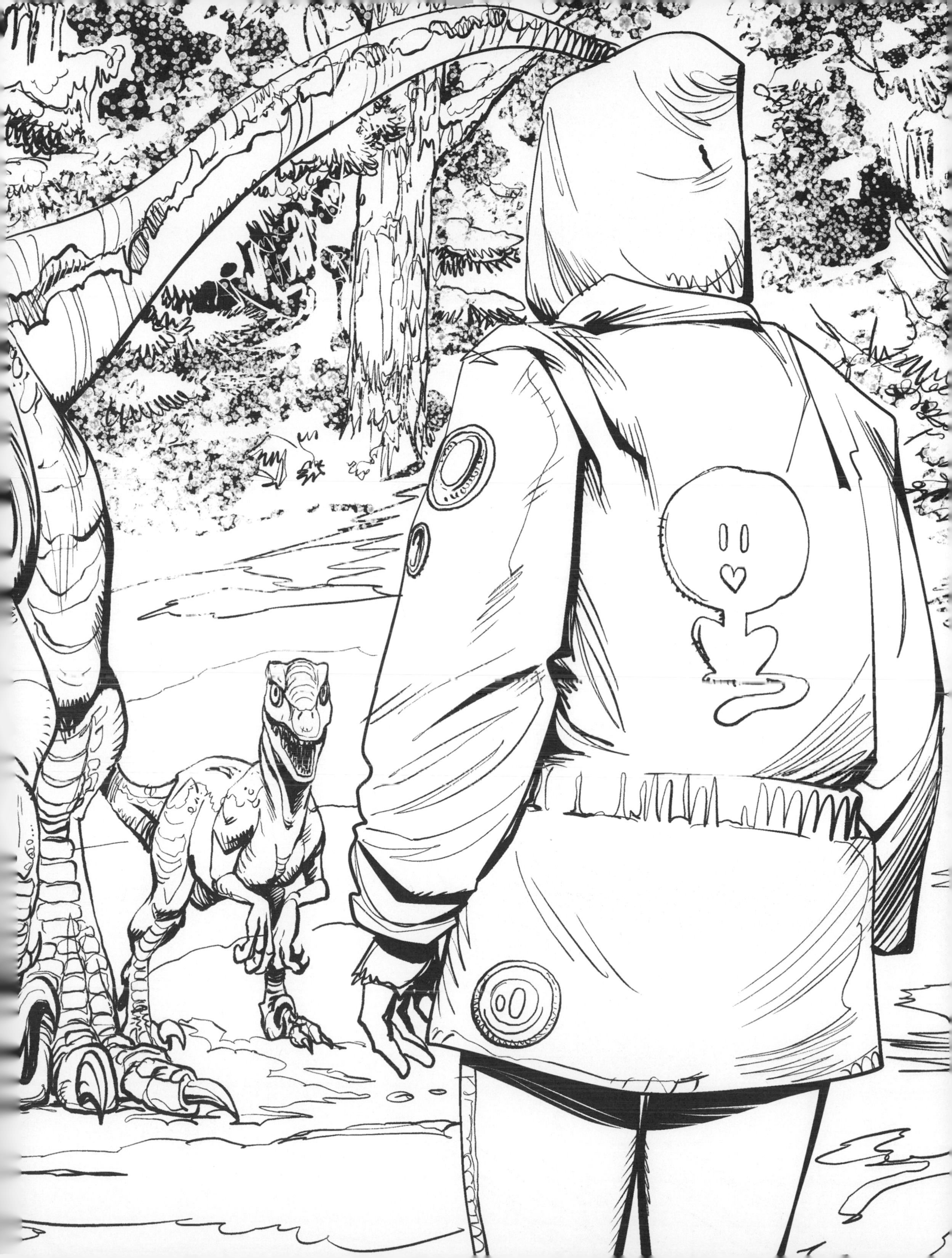

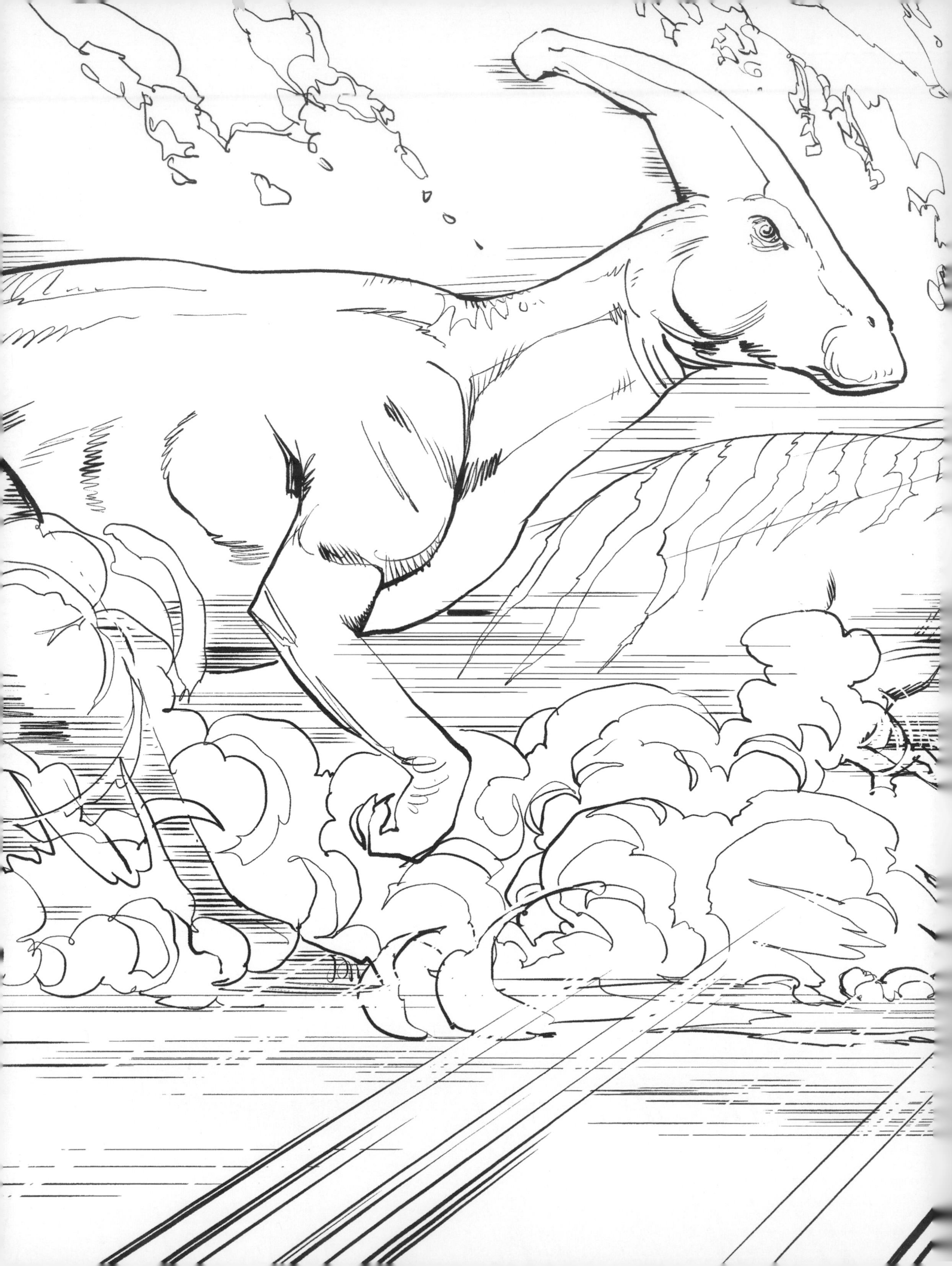

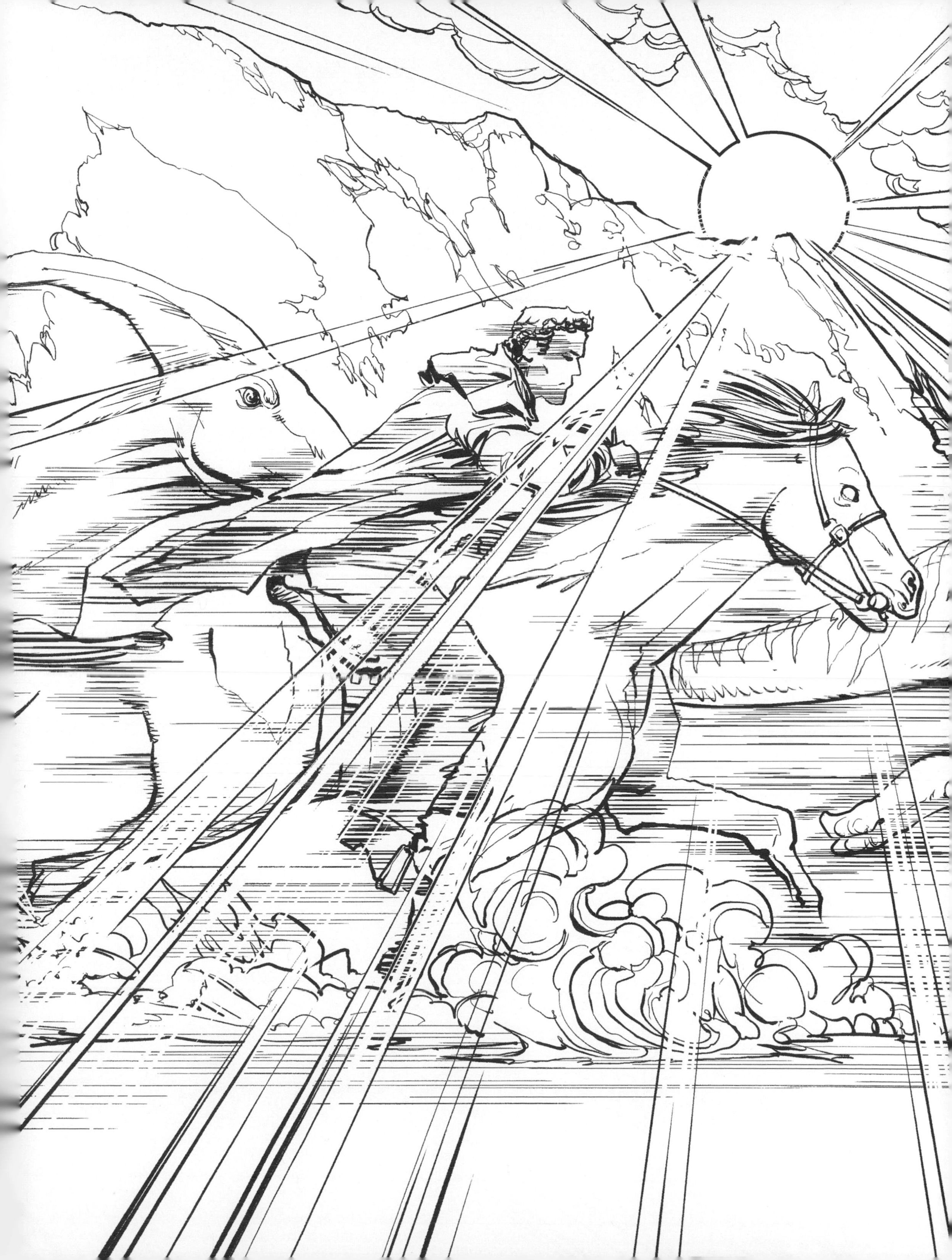

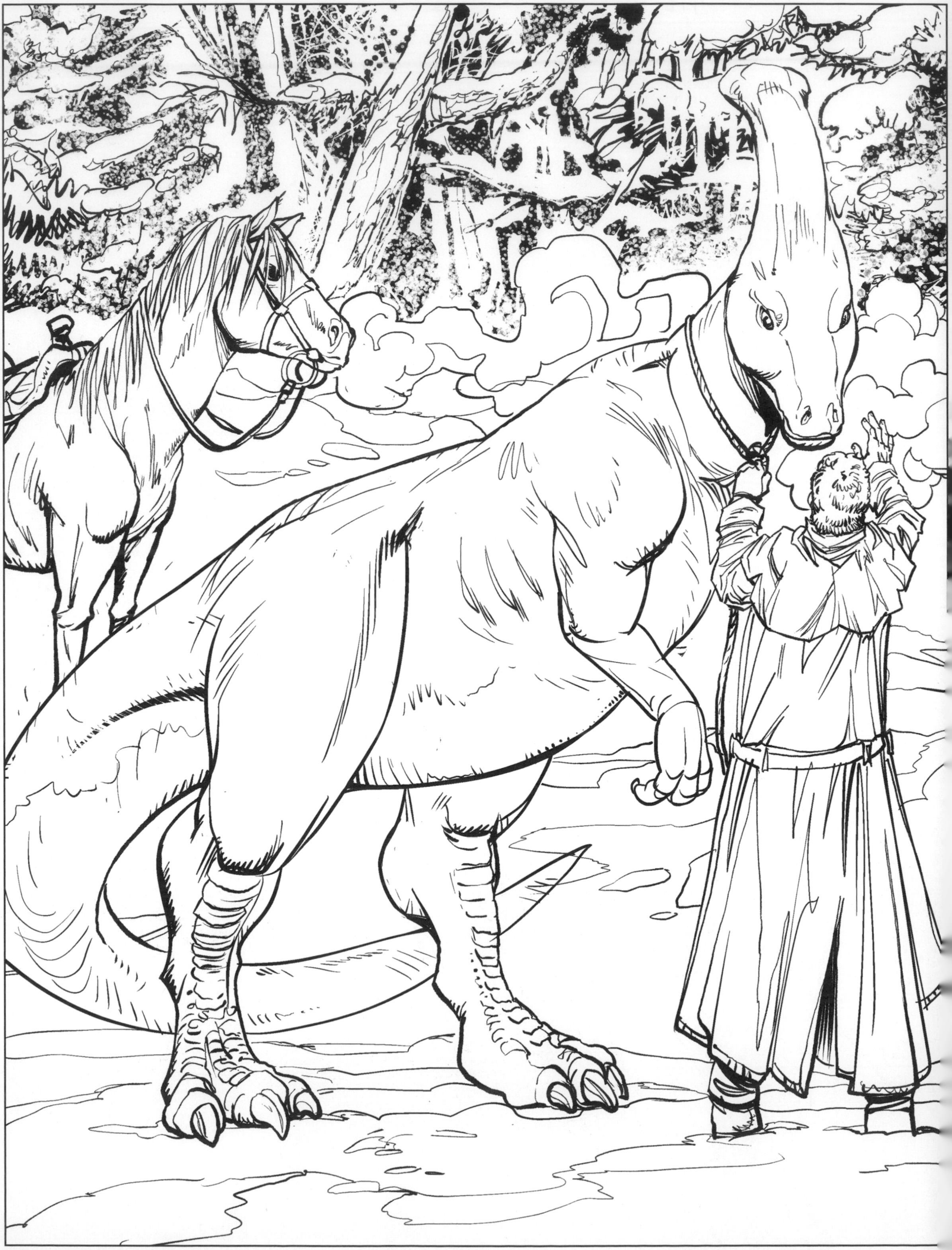

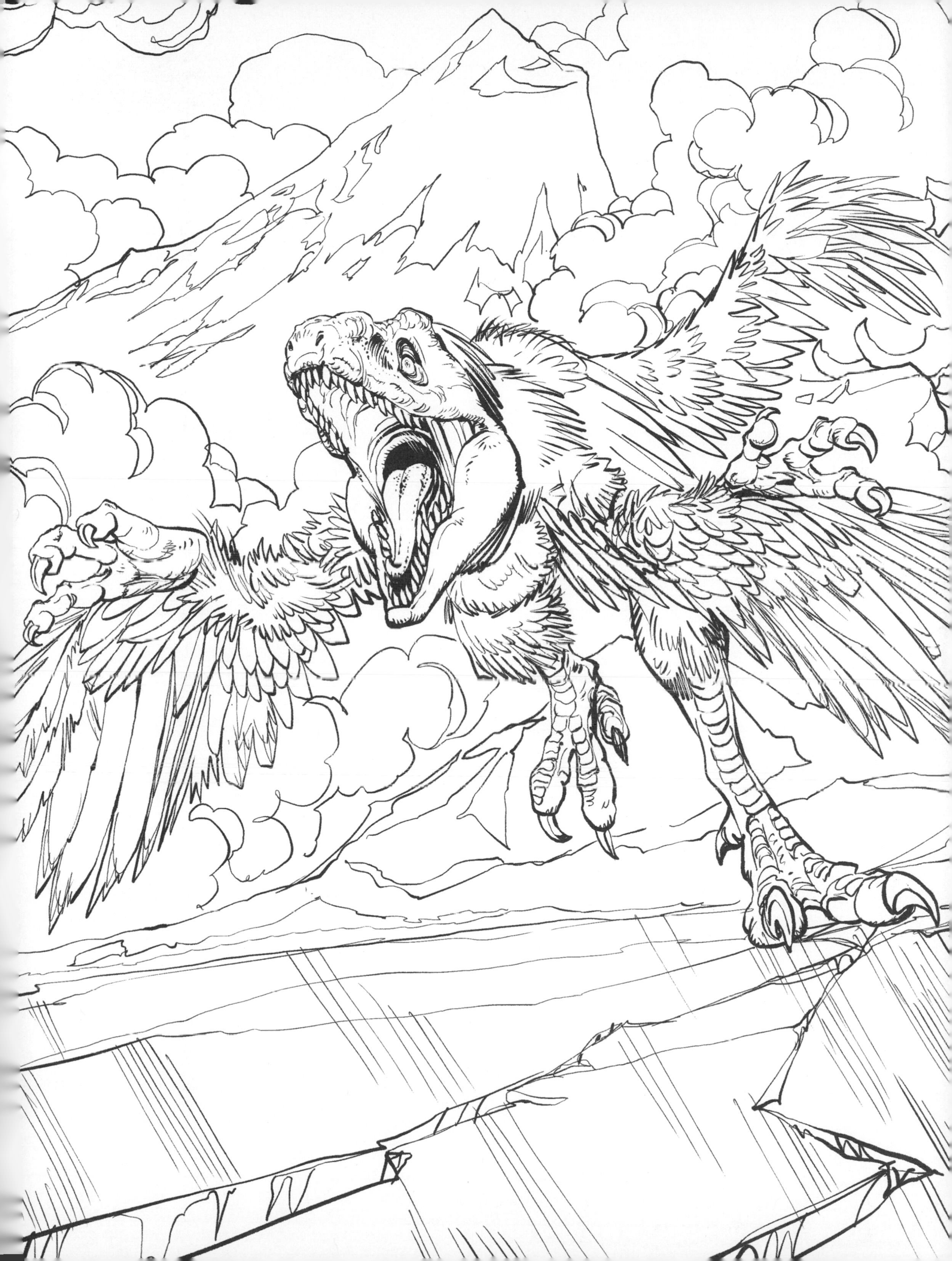

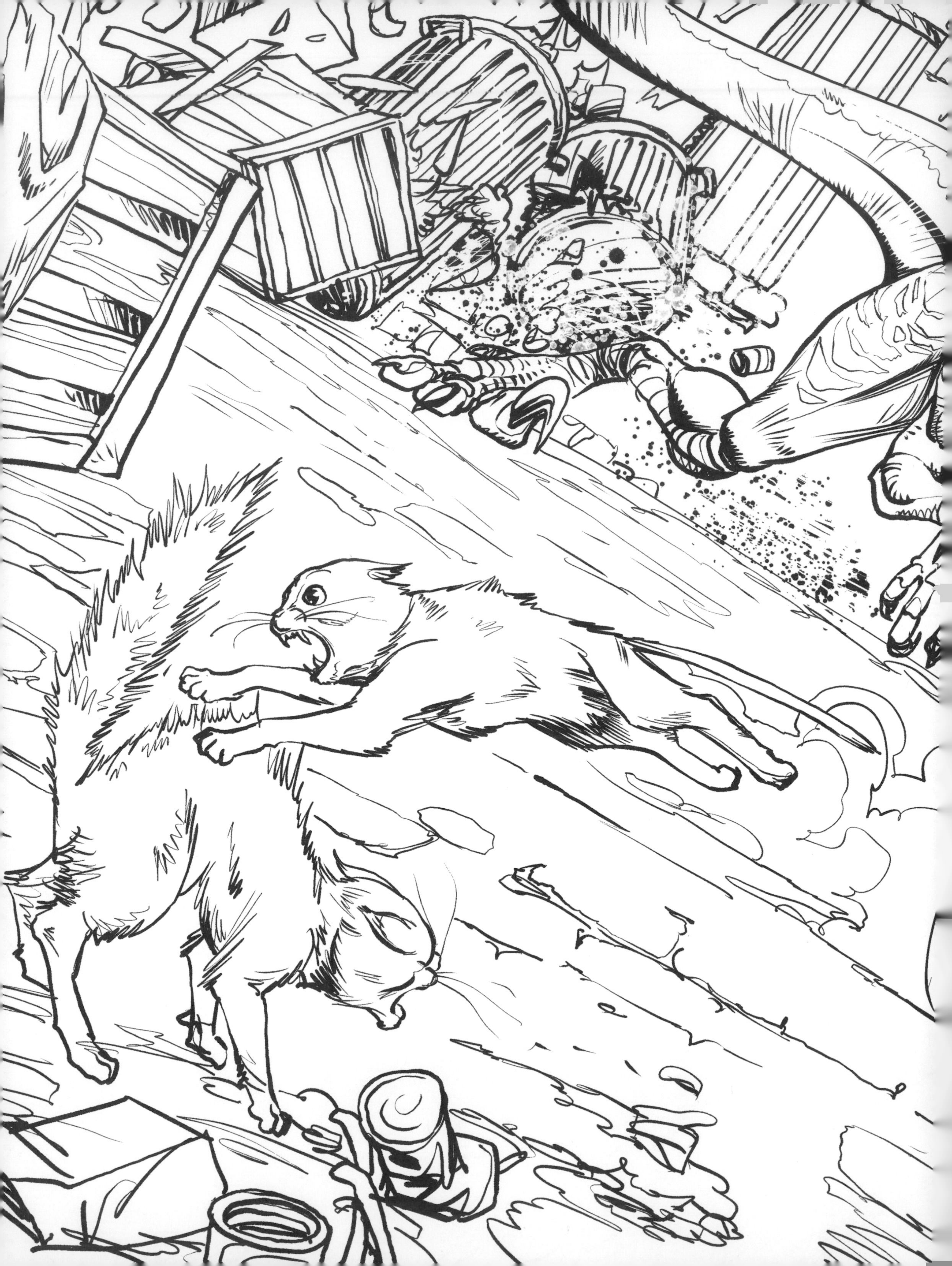

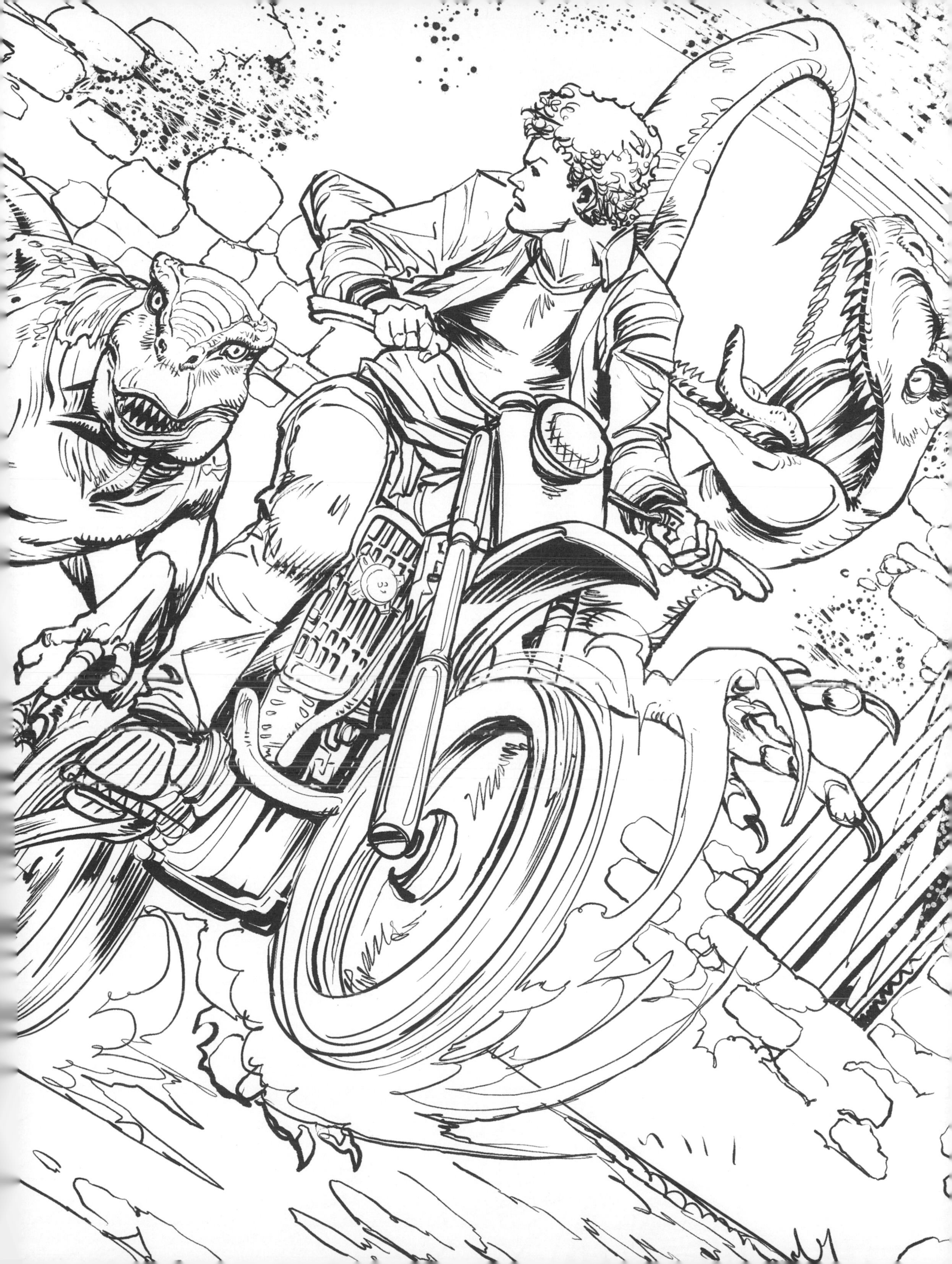

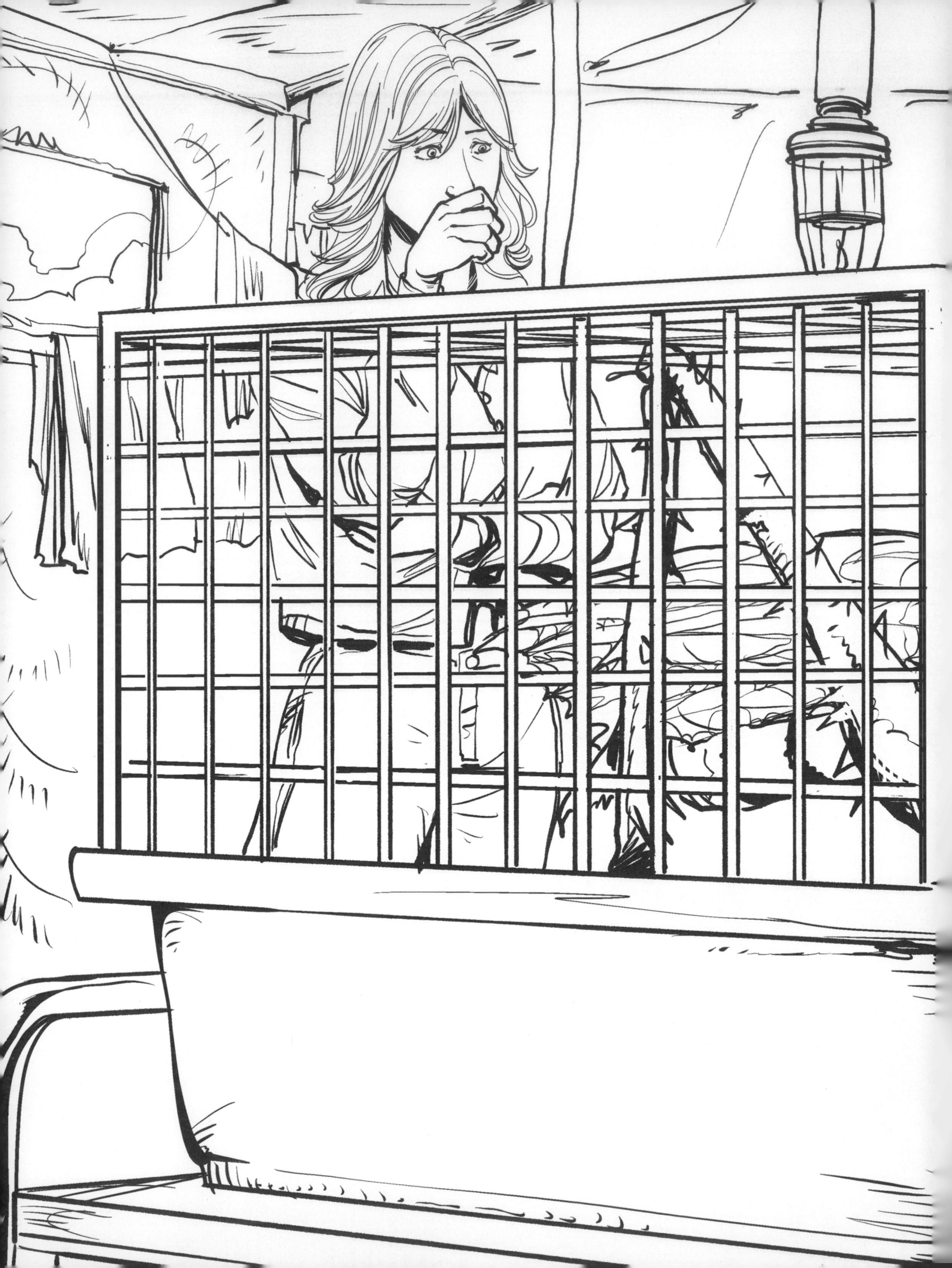

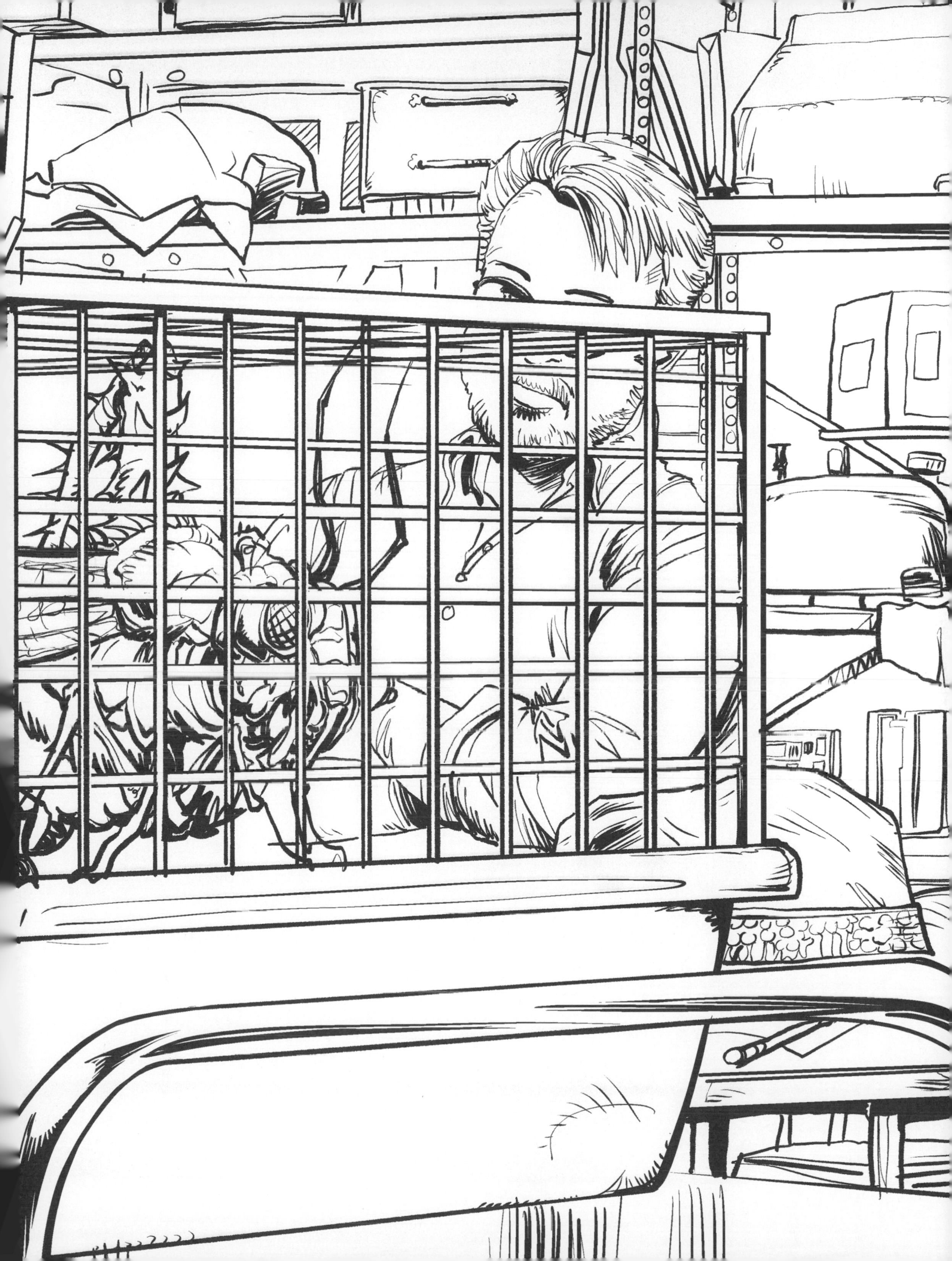

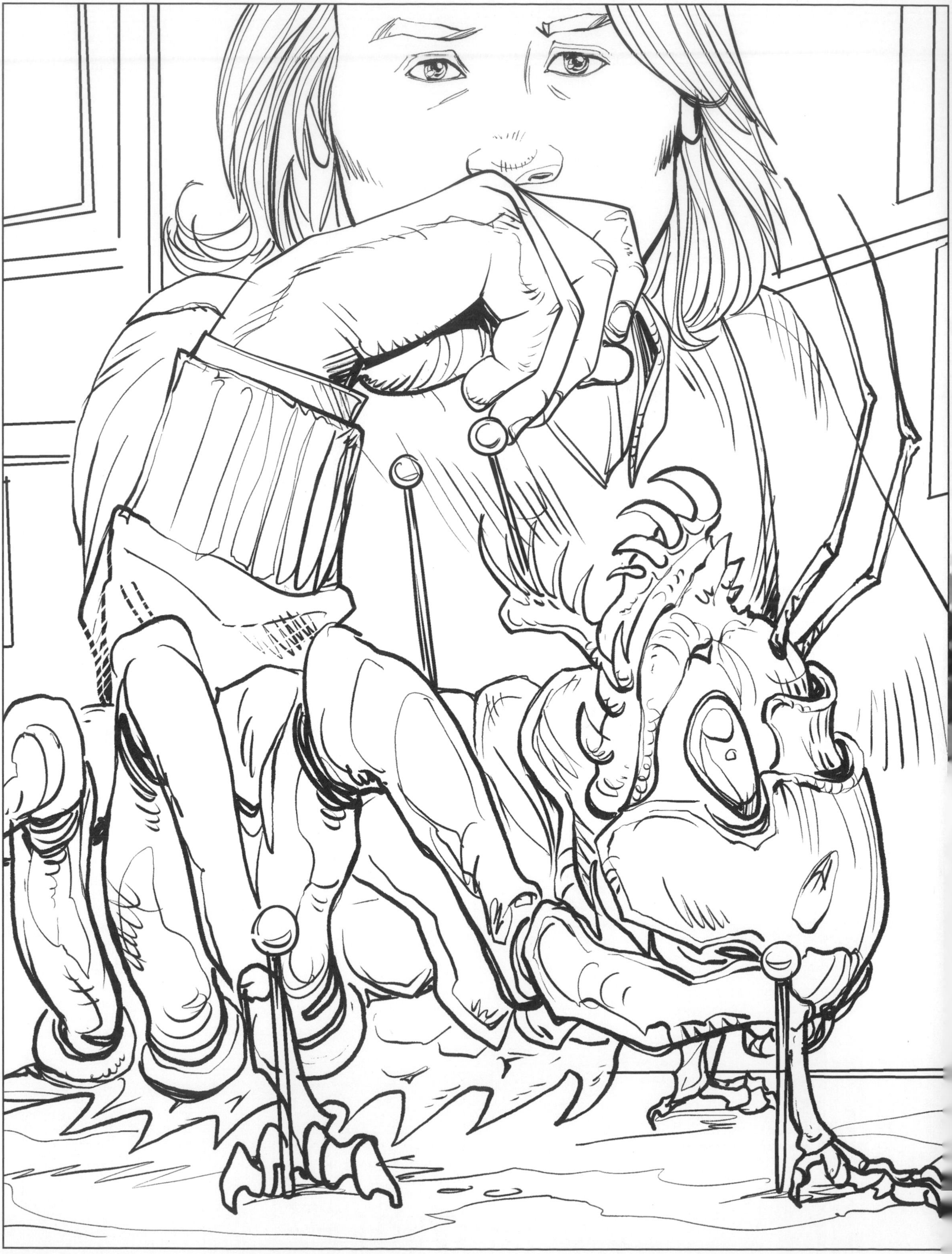

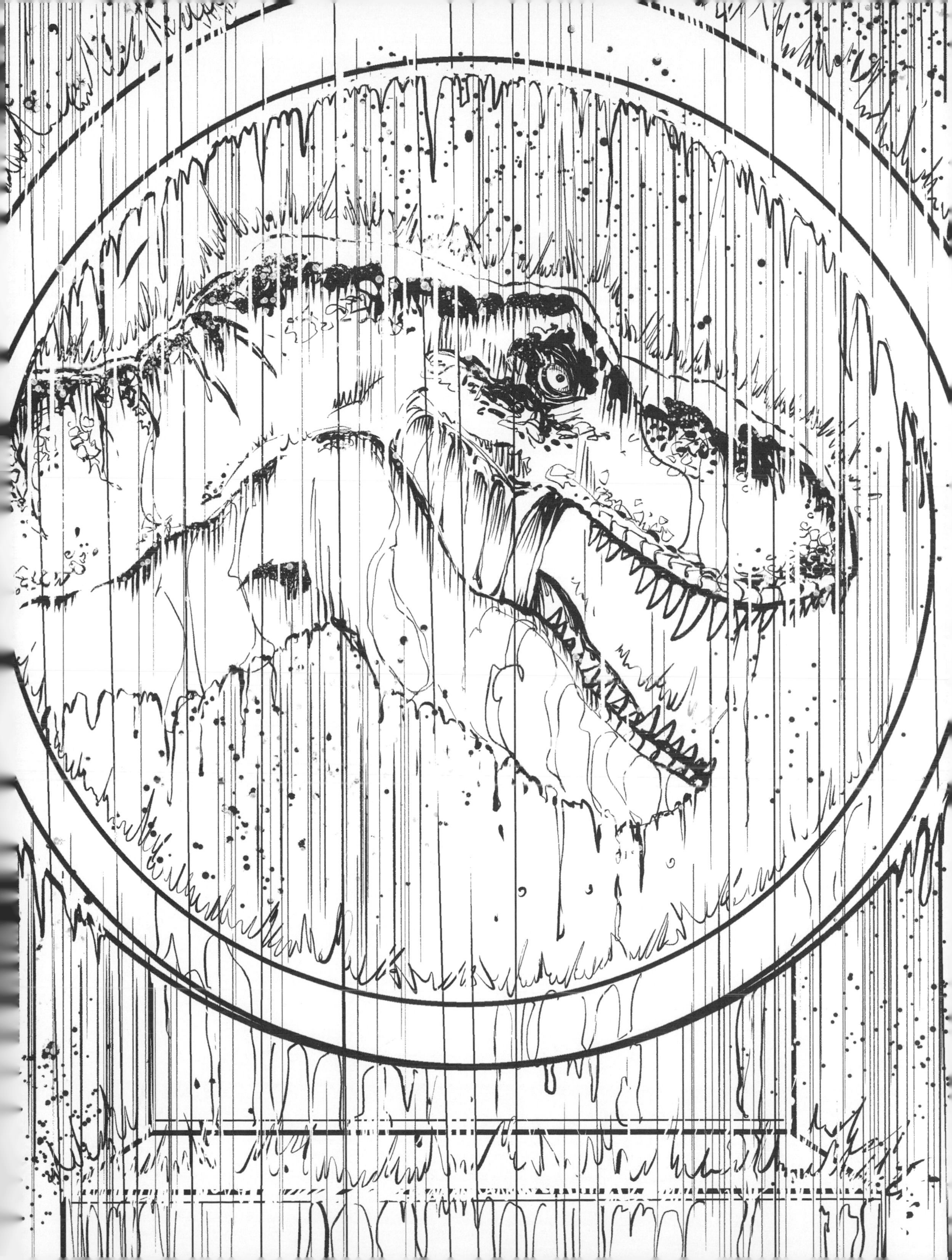

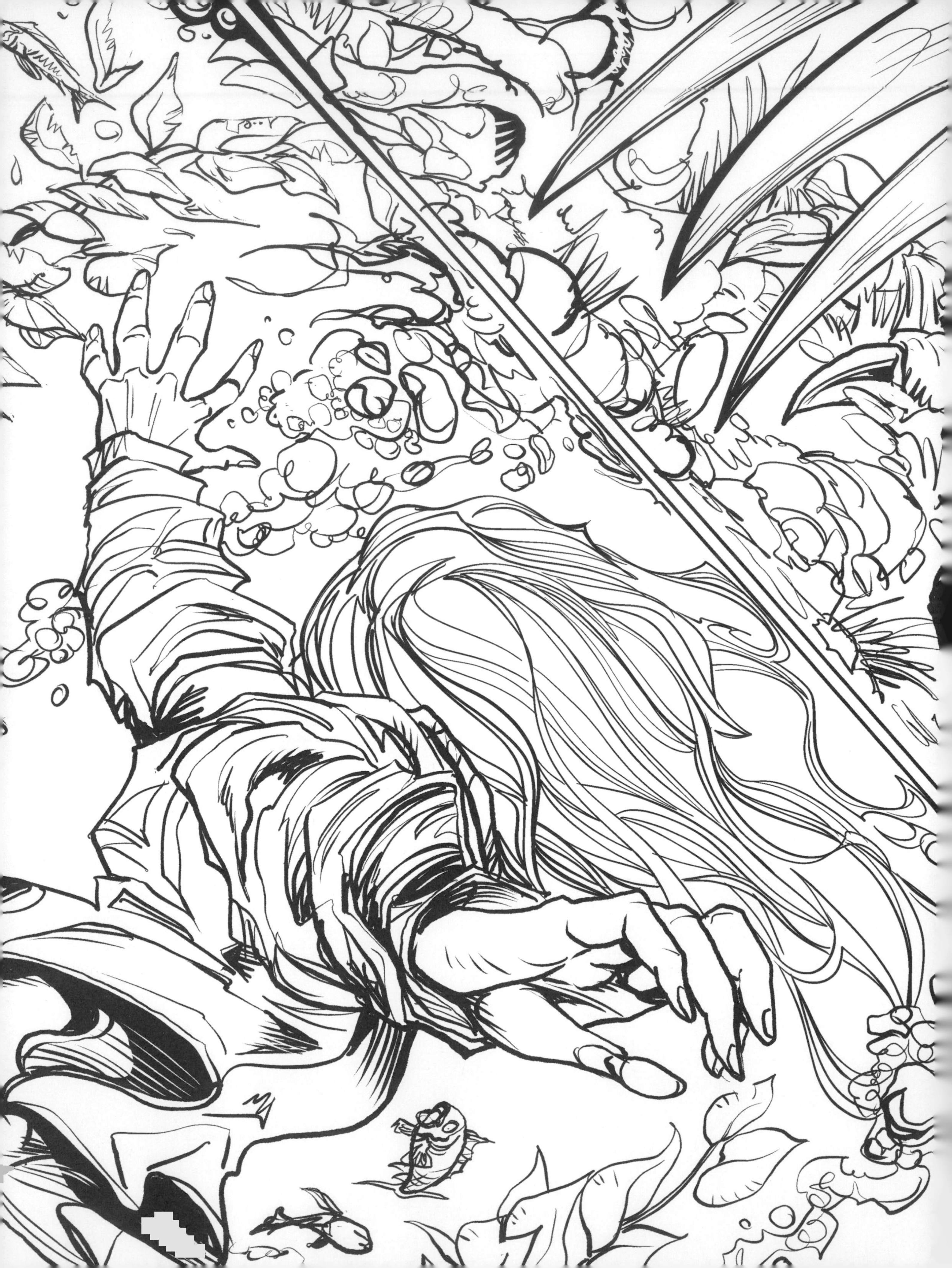

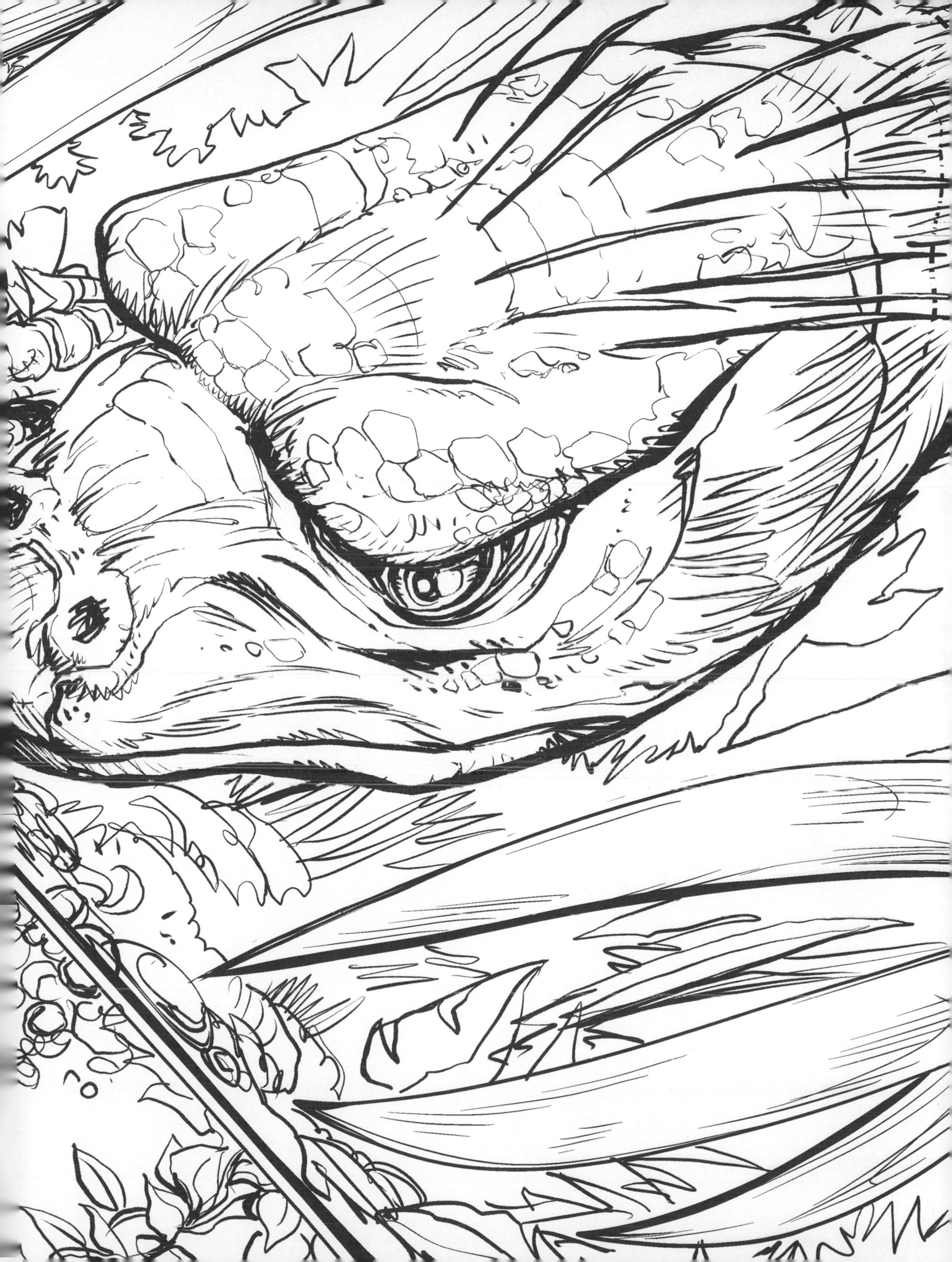

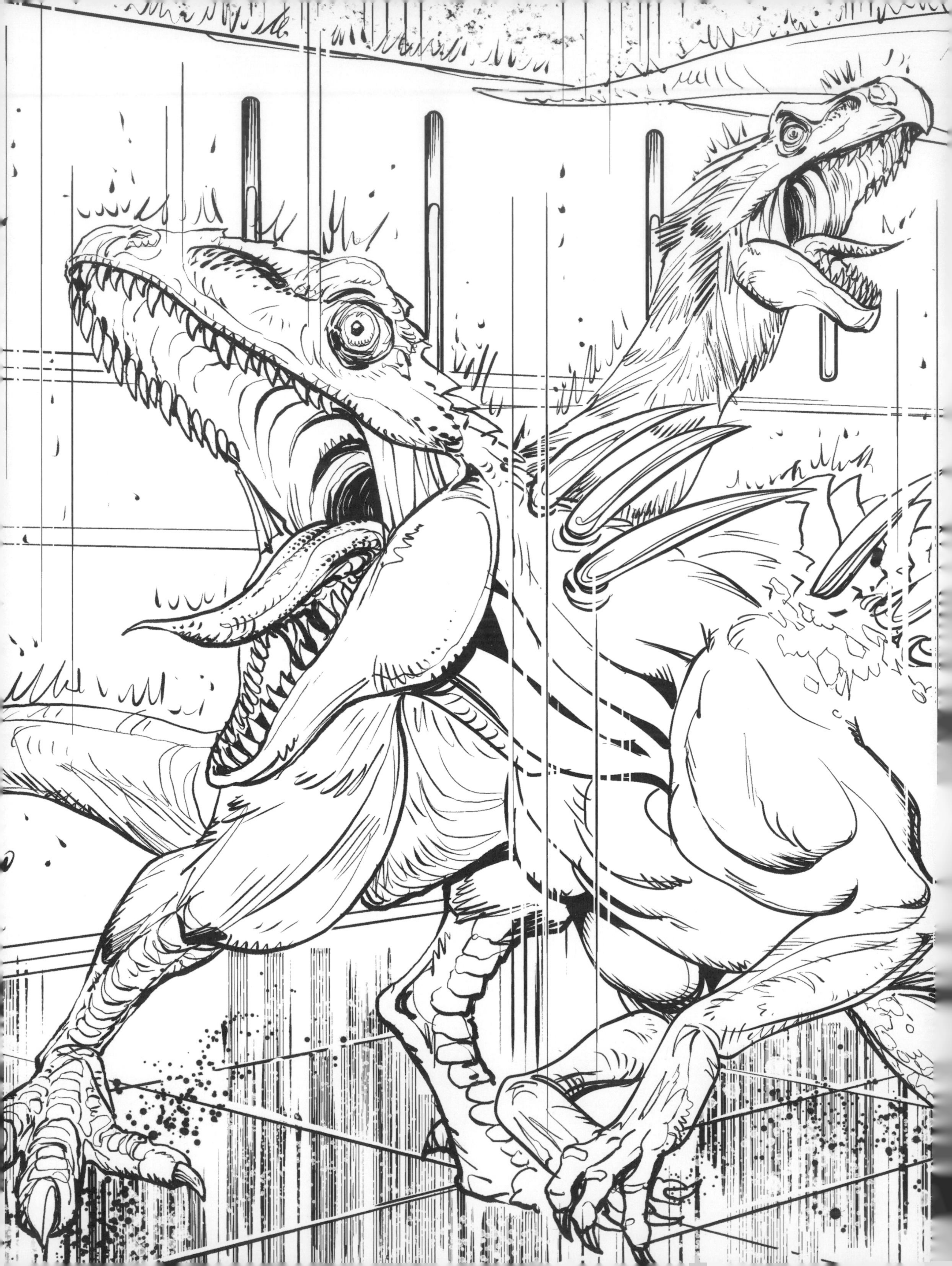

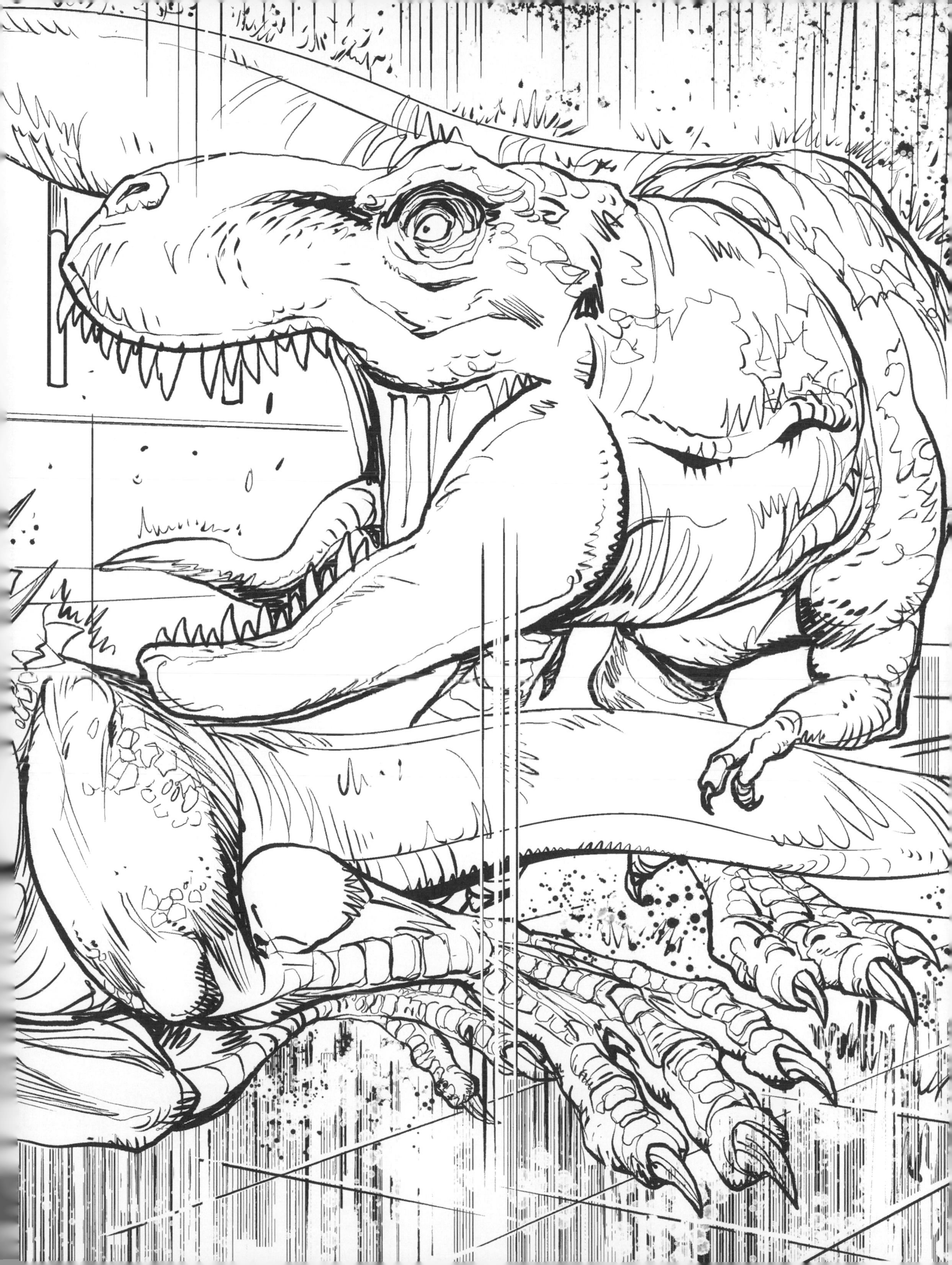

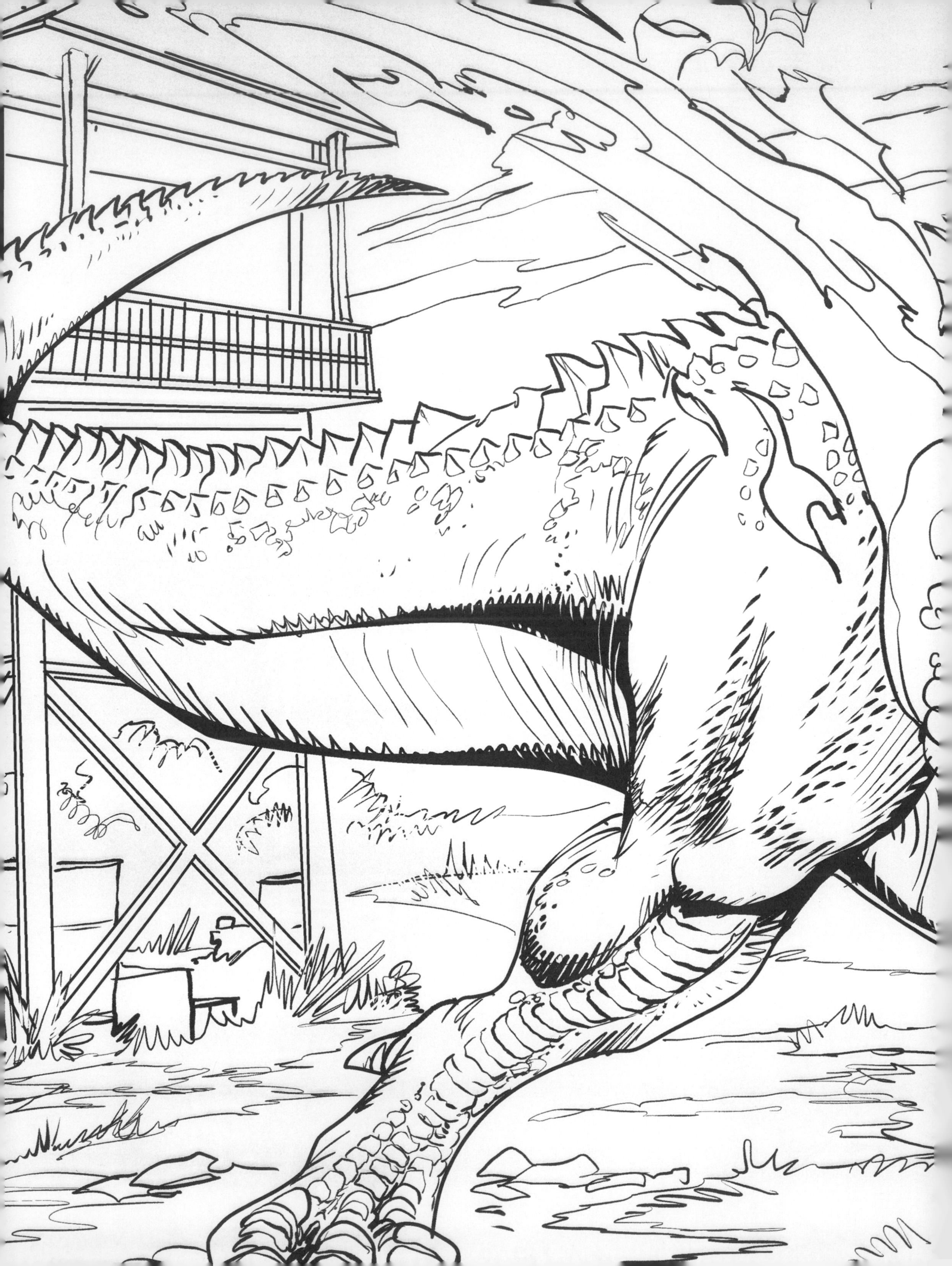

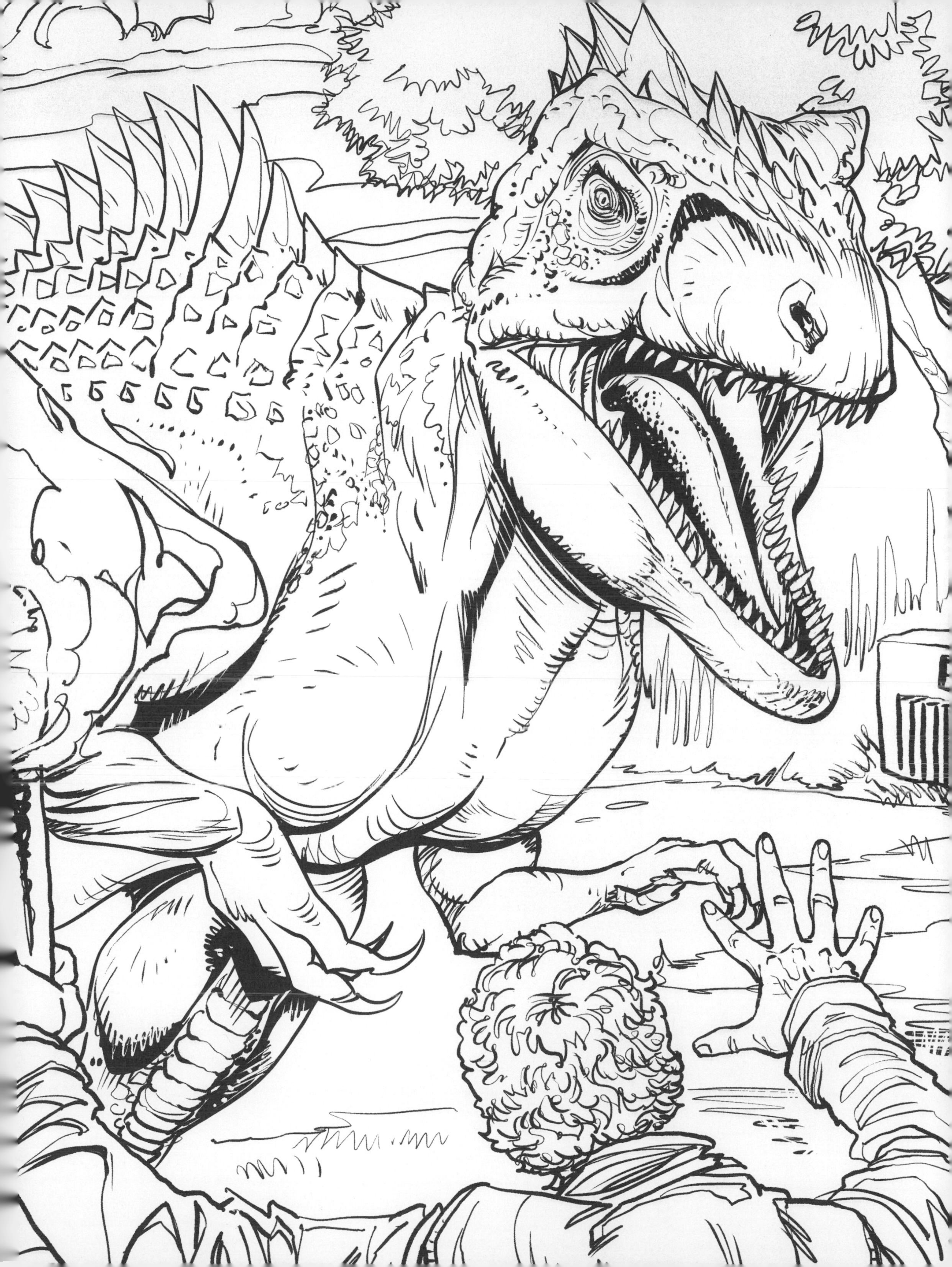

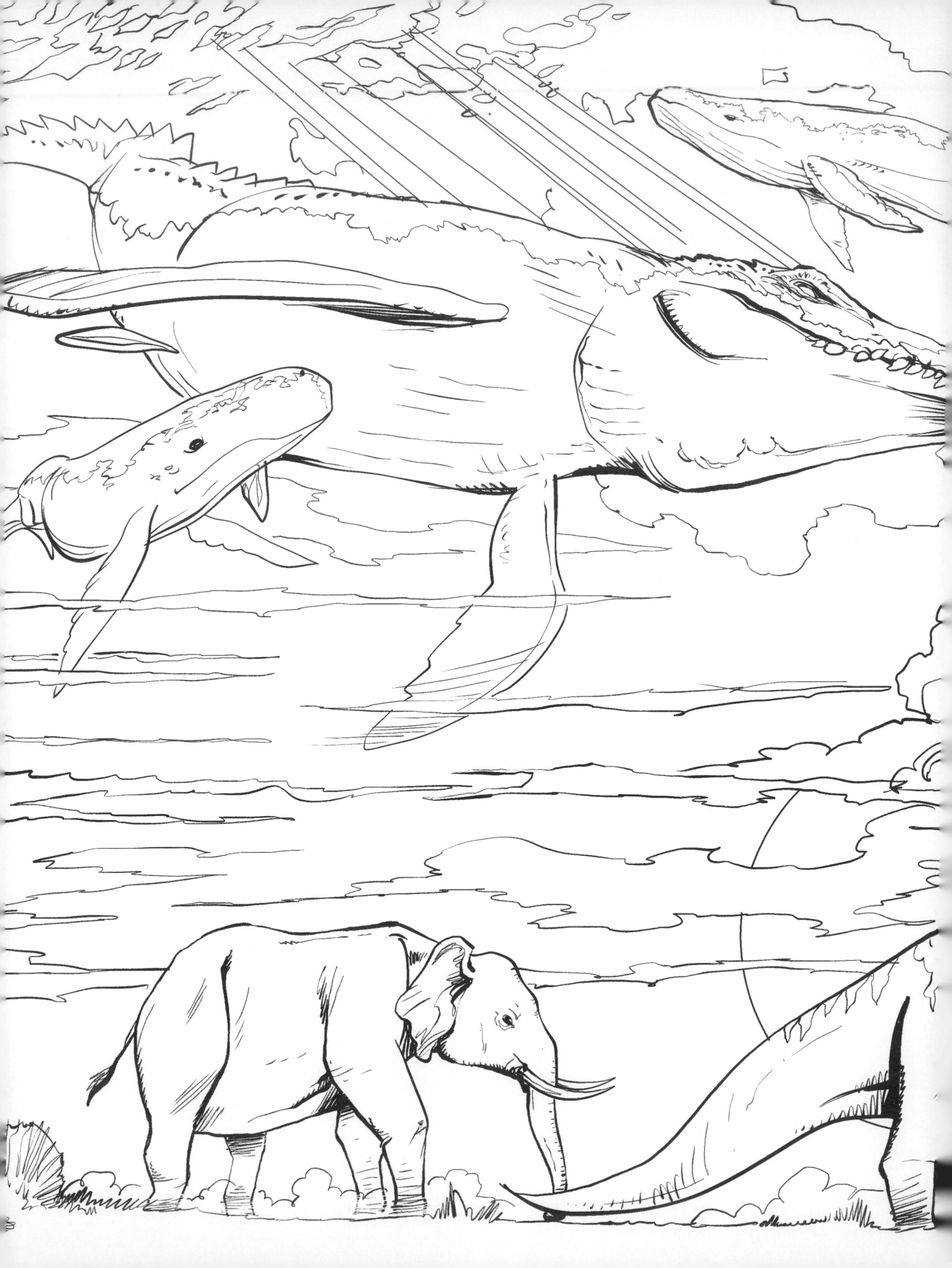

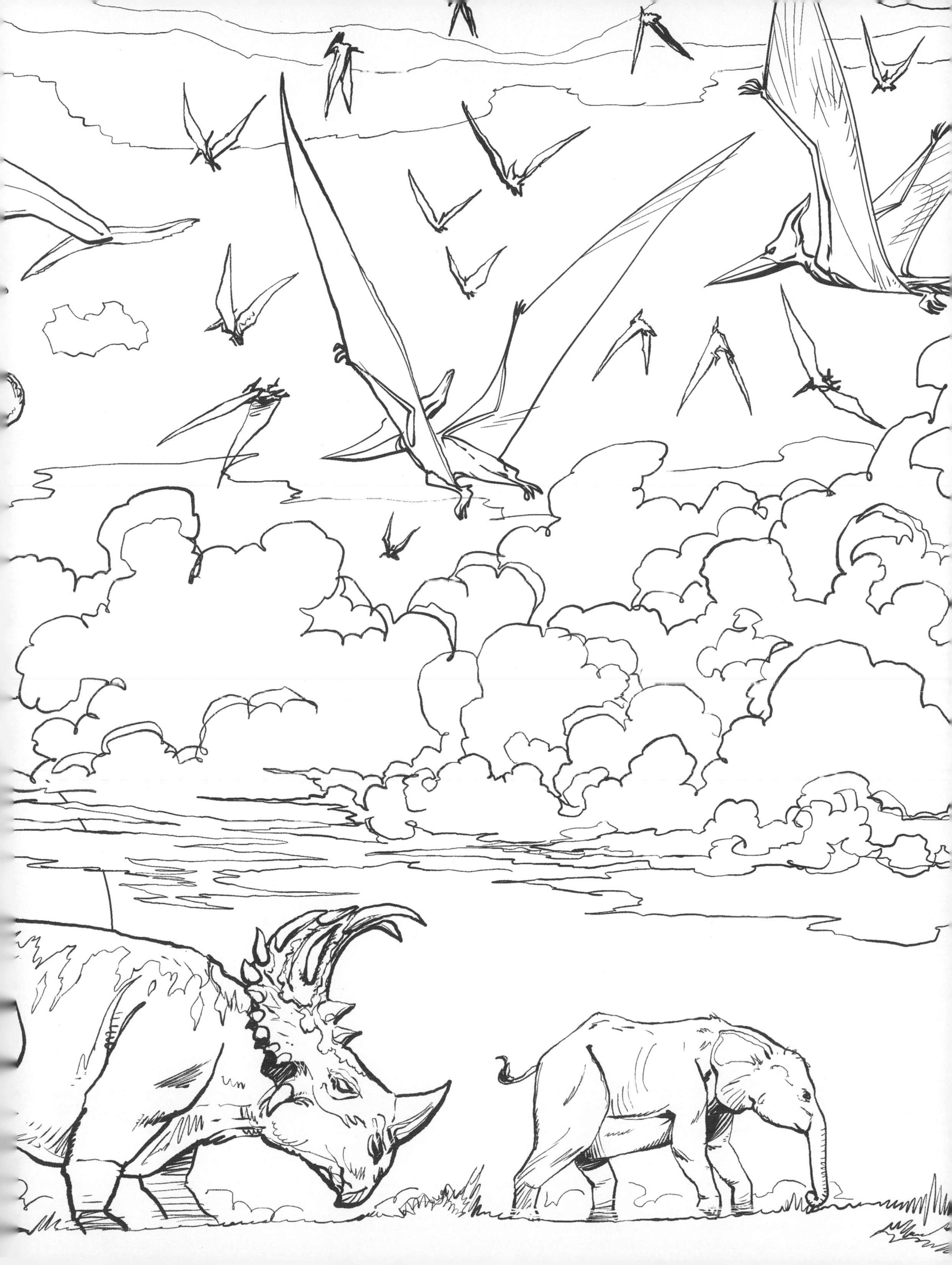

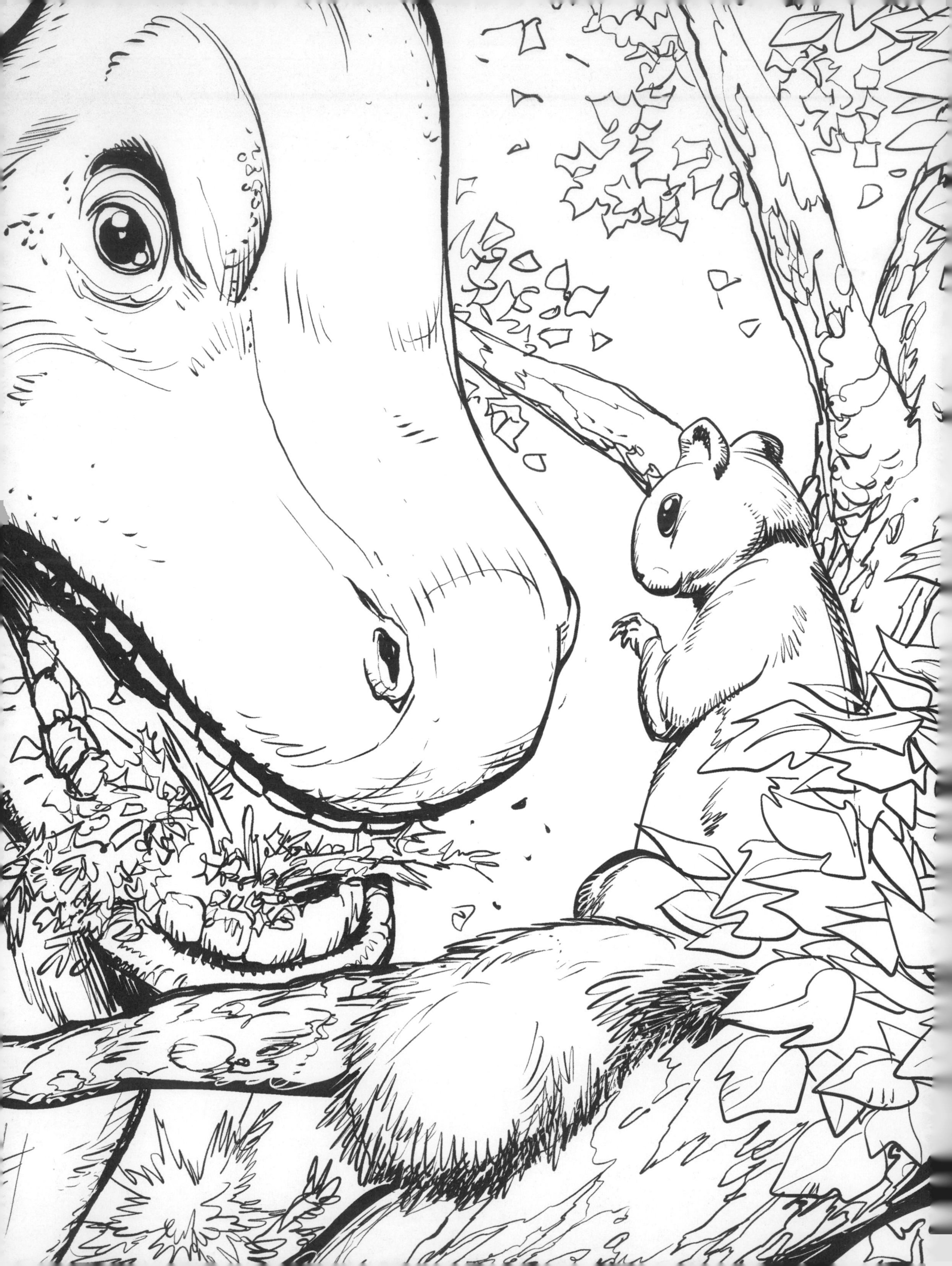